James Johonnot

Neighbors with Claws and Hoofs

And their Kin

James Johonnot

Neighbors with Claws and Hoofs
And their Kin

ISBN/EAN: 9783337059583

Printed in Europe, USA, Canada, Australia, Japan

Cover: Foto ©ninafisch / pixelio.de

More available books at **www.hansebooks.com**

NATURAL HISTORY SERIES—BOOK FOURTH.

NEIGHBORS WITH
CLAWS AND HOOFS,

AND

THEIR KIN.

FOR BOYS AND GIRLS.

By JAMES JOHONNOT.

NEW YORK .:. CINCINNATI .:. CHICAGO:
AMERICAN BOOK COMPANY.

"The crows flapped over by twos and threes,
 In the pool drowsed the cattle up to their knees,
  The little birds sang as if it were
   The one day of summer of all the year,
 And the very leaves seemed to sing on the trees."

COPYRIGHT, 1885,
BY D. APPLETON AND COMPANY.

THE METHOD AND THE REASON FOR IT.

As pupils advance toward maturity they are not satisfied with such facts and obvious relations as have been the delight of their childhood. Their minds crave something that lies beyond the world of sense. Reflective energies begin to assert themselves, forming a balance for the perceptives. The when, the where, and the how no longer engross the attention, and the why comes into prominence. Observation and experiment have brought into life mental desires which extend beyond individual experience, and which find their satisfaction only in the accumulated experiences of the race.

To furnish a solid basis for thought, pupils just entering this reflective age still need the facts which observation gives. To satisfy the cravings of their new-born energies, and to stimulate their powers to greater activity, they also need the results of general human investigation as recorded in science and literature. Upon such food the mind feeds and grows.

This book is specially prepared for minds in the transition state here indicated. The facts given are stated in such a way as to lead to more careful observation, while the relations presented reach up toward the laws and principles which govern things. The subject-matter embraces the highest orders of animal life and organism in its most complex forms; its investigation equally calling into exercise the perceptive and reflective powers.

As in the other members of the series, the method of the book is inductive. Each division of the subject begins with the representative animal that is nearest home and most familiar. The cat at the fireside serves as an introduction to the lion and tiger and other cats of the wilds; the kin of the faithful dog is traced in wolf and jackal; and rats and rabbits represent rodents the world over. From the sty, the stable, and the farm-yard, the mind travels out to the homes of the rhinoceros, the elephant, and the buffalo, in desert, plain, and jungle.

The steps of this route are those of comparison. The imagination is aroused and disciplined. The pictures impressed upon the mind are almost as vivid as those obtained from direct perception. A taste is developed for scientific research, and a fair preparation is made for successful scientific study.

A few fables and stories of the folk-lore kind have been selected to show how animals have been regarded in the past, and how their traits have been used to illustrate and enforce moral lessons. These fables are of such universal application as to be fresh with each generation of children for all time.

CONTENTS.

CHAPTER		PAGE
I.	Cats of Forest and Prairie	11
II.	Cats of Desert and Jungle	17
III.	The King of the Tropical Wilds	22
IV.	The Sultana of the Desert	27
V.	The Guardians of the Household	34
VI.	Trained and Faithful Servants	40
VII.	"Our Beloved Brother Prince"	46
VIII.	Savage Dogs of Forest and Plain	50
IX.	Sly-Boots	54
X.	Slyer than a Fox	61
XI.	Pests of the Household	66
XII.	The Legend of Bishop Hatto	74
XIII.	Nut-Crackers and Wood-Cutters	77
XIV.	Long Ears and their Kin	85
XV.	Bird-Language	91
XVI.	The Monarch of the Mountain	92
XVII.	How I killed a Bear	102
XVIII.	The Bear in Fable and Story	108
XIX.	Our Servants of Stable and Harness	117
XX.	Kaweah's Run	123
XXI.	The Alarm Bell of Atri	130
XXII.	Swine and their Forest Cousins	134
XXIII.	The Arab's Story of a Boar	139
XXIV.	Giants with Tusks and Trunk	143

CONTENTS.—(Continued.)

CHAPTER		PAGE
XXV.	The Monarch of African Waters	151
XXVI.	The Giant Pig of the Jungle	157
XXVII.	The Fiftieth Birthday of Agassiz	162
XXVIII.	Our Farm-Yard Milk-Givers	164
XXIX.	The Bovine Dwellers of Other Lands	171
XXX.	The Rodeo of the Llanos	178
XXXI.	Wool-Bearers of the Pastures	184
XXXII.	Mountain Milk-Givers	190
XXXIII.	Agile Dwellers of Mountain and Plain	195
XXXIV.	Antlered Tenants of the Woods	203
XXXV.	The Laplander's Treasure	210
XXXVI.	The Ship of the Desert	215
XXXVII.	Some Cousins of the Camel	222
XXXVIII.	Foot-handed Foxes and Squirrels	229
XXXIX.	Howlers and Weepers of Amazonian Forests	233
XL.	Long-tailed Dwellers of the Tree-Tops	241
XLI.	Tailless Tree-Climbers of the Wilds	246

THE FOX AND THE GRAPES.

A hungry fox saw some ripe clusters of grapes hanging high up on a vine. He leaped upward, and for a long time tried to get at them. Finding them beyond his reach, and tired out with jumping, he limped off and said, "Just as I thought—those grapes are sour!"

The Jaguar.

CHAPTER I.

CATS OF FOREST AND PRAIRIE.

1. As our old friend the cat lies stretched before the fire or moves about the house, we can give attention to her peculiar eye that adapts itself to darkness as well as light; to her cushioned paws that enable her to tread softly and noiselessly as if on velvet; to her five toes on her fore-paws, and four toes on her hind-paws; to the sharp claws with which these toes are armed, which are thrust out of sheaths when needed for use, and withdrawn and covered when at rest. We can also notice the incisor or cutting teeth of the cat, of which she has six above and six below; and the four canine or dog teeth, so much longer than the rest, which she possesses in common with nearly all other carnivorous or flesh-eating animals.

2. All these curious things about a cat should be carefully borne in mind, because they are possessed by the numerous species of the cat kind, and bring into close cousinship the mouser that purrs on the warm hearth and the lion that wakes the echoes in the African forest; and this same relationship of the home cat lends a new interest to all her habits. To see her walk softly, stealthily crouching half-way to the ground, and gracefully curling back and forth her long tail as she draws near to and finally springs upon her prey, is to see just what the jaguar, leopard, tiger, or other greater cats do.

3. The wild cat, which is twice as large as the home cat, "is common to almost every country, and is celebrated for its ferocity. It is distinguishable from the domestic cat not only by its greater size, but by the shortness of its tail, which shows that it is of another species.

4. "The wild cat makes its nest in hollow trees near the ground, and is so ingenious in disguising its location that it is rarely discovered. It is very successful in its

The Wild Cat.

search for food, and every species of bird and small quadruped becomes its prey. When it once discovers a flock of wild turkeys, it will keep in the vicinity until the young and inexperienced are destroyed. The wild cat of America is different from that of Europe, and is a cousin of the lynx.

5. "In the early settlement of Kentucky a schoolmaster was sitting alone in his log-cabin, when he was surprised to see a large cat enter his premises. Ignorant of the ferocity of this wild animal, he shut the door and commenced an attack. The battle was long and bloody,

the man being torn nearly into shreds; and when discovered in the morning he was found with his hands upon the cat's throat, his knees upon its haunches, the animal dead and stiffened by cold. The victor, in his terror, had probably remained in the position described the livelong night, his muscles paralyzed, his nerves shattered, and never through a long life did he entirely recover from the terrible encounter."

6. The jaguar is a native of tropical South America, and of North America as far north as Louisiana. It very closely resembles the leopard. The spots on its skin are rings of dark color, inclosing spaces of lighter hue, and resemble rosettes. It is sometimes called the American tiger. "It follows in the tracks of wild herds of cattle and horses, and thus finds its principal subsistence. Its mode of killing prey differs from that of the other cats, which is to seize by the throat. The jaguar, on the contrary, springs upon the back of its victim, and by its arms and with a sudden jerk of the head dislocates the neck. Its strength is sufficient to enable it to drag the body of a horse a great distance.

7. "It is related that, many years ago, a jaguar took possession of a church at Santa Fé and killed the padre. The priest's absence caused suspicion, and an assistant went to the church, but to the people was as unaccountably delayed as his predecessor. After some time another priest entered the church, and was instantly attacked by the jaguar; but he managed to escape and give the alarm. No one now could be found brave enough to enter the building; so the people unroofed a corner of the church, and from a safe distance shot their enemy.

8. "The puma is the American lion; at least it bears a closer resemblance to that noble beast than any other of the feline family, for it is destitute of the stripes of the

tiger, the spots of the leopard, and the rosettes of the jaguar; but the full-grown animal possesses a tawny-red color, almost uniform over the whole body, and hence the inference that it is like the lion. In different parts of the country it has been called by different names, as panther, or 'painter,' and mountain-lion, or cougar. The true panther is a different animal, and lives in Africa.

The Puma and Deer.

9. "In form the puma is less attractive than the generality of its species, there being an apparent want of symmetry. Its back is hollow, its legs short and thick, and its tail does not gracefully taper. Yet Nature has given to the puma other qualities as a compensation, the most remarkable of which is its power to render itself quite invisible; for so cunningly tinged is its fur, that it perfectly mingles with the bark of trees, and, stretched out upon a limb, or even extended upon the floor of its dimly-lighted cage, it is difficult to be assured of its presence.

10. "A hunter on the Rio Grande, who was always successful, became so annoyed by the taunts of his companions that he determined to adopt the Comanche Indian fashion of hunting, and accordingly dressed himself in a deer-skin and ornamented his head with huge antlers.

Thus equipped he sallied out and took his place at a favorite 'stand.' A few moments only elapsed before a puma, perched in the limbs of the tree above, thinking that he saw a 'sure-enough buck,' leaped from his airy abode plump on the hunter's back, at the same time burying his claws and teeth deeply into the dried skin.

11. "A yell of fright and astonishment greeted the puma such as never before was heard from the throat of living venison, and, dropping his game, the animal and the hunter took different directions, it being a matter of uncertainty even to this day which of the two was most alarmed."

12. The lynx is a spotted animal, abounding in the northern parts of Europe, Asia, and America. It varies in size, some species being nearly as large as a wolf. The ancients consecrated this animal to Bacchus, and Pliny tells about it some absurd stories, among which is that it can see through a wall. Hence the expression lynx-eyed, denoting keen sight, which has passed into our language.

The Lynx.

This animal frequents mountains and wooded districts, hunting in pairs, the female frequently followed by her young. He reposes during the day, and goes forth by night to seek his prey.

13. The hyena is not so much of a cat as the animals

already described. His feet are all four-toed; his body slopes back from the shoulders; his neck wears a bushy mane. In disposition and appetite he is ferocious and ravenous, and he can not be tamed. Bruce says of the hyena, in his "Travels": "We have no reason to attribute

The Hyena.

extraordinary wisdom to him. He is, on the contrary, brutish, indolent, slovenly, and impudent, and seems to possess the manners of the wolf. His courage has nothing of the brave in it, and he dies oftener flying than fighting.

14. "In Barbary I have seen the Moors in the daytime take this animal by the ears and pull him toward them without his attempting any other resistance than that of drawing back; and the hunters, when his cave is large enough to give them admittance, take a torch in their hand and go straight to him, when they throw a blanket over him and drag him out."

CHAPTER II.

CATS OF DESERT AND JUNGLE.

1. "The leopard," says Anderssen, "is common throughout Southern Africa generally, but, from its cunning, active nature, and nocturnal habits, is but rarely seen. It is

The Leopard.

about two feet seven inches high at the shoulder, and seven feet six inches in extreme length. The chin, neck, breast, and inside of the extremities, are white, the rest tawny or reddish-brown, irregularly marked with spots of black, which vary in number, size, and appearance, at different ages and seasons. In its wild state it is exceedingly beautiful, its motions in the highest degree easy and graceful, and its agility in bounding among the rocks and woods quite amazing.

2. "The chief resorts of the leopard are mountainous districts where rock is piled on rock in frightful confusion, leaving between them fissures and caverns. It is

met also in dense brakes and tangled coverts, where, if hard pressed by the hunter, it takes refuge in a tree, and, if this be large and thickly shaded, it is not without difficulty that the animal is discovered, it having a marvelous faculty of concealing itself behind some knotty branch or at the junction of the larger limbs with the trunk.

3. "Its food is various; indeed, hardly anything comes amiss to its voracious appetite and blood-thirsty nature, and, what is worse, it wantonly slays more than it can eat, and thus becomes doubly destructive. It attacks birds, monkeys, baboons, dogs, antelopes, sheep, goats, and young cattle. It is said that it causes the natives and colonists more damage than even the lion and other beasts of prey put together. It preys upon the ostrich, among whose kind, from their want of smell and sight, it commits great ravages. I am inclined to believe that of the large number annually destroyed, whether by man or otherwise, two thirds may be fairly charged to the leopard's account. I was, on a certain occasion, an eye-witness to its wonderful powers in this way. It was under these circumstances:

4. "One evening a little before sunset, while I was still suffering from the effects of fever, all my dogs suddenly began to give chase to some animal which the distance did not enable me to distinguish. Judging from their movements, however, they had a formidable antagonist before them. They were, I concluded, from their steady, unbroken, deep bay, close upon the haunches of the enemy, yet I could not distinctly see either the dogs or the object of their pursuit.

5. "All at once a magnificent leopard sprang right before me from the topmost branches of a tall acacia, clearing with a single bound all his fierce assailants. I was so astounded at the magnitude of the leap that, looking first at the tree and then at the place on which the beautiful

animal alighted, I could hardly withdraw my eyes from the spot. Had the dogs been equally fascinated they would have lost their prey, but, spurred on by rage, before the leopard had run a hundred yards they had overpowered and killed him."

6. "Naturalists are not very well agreed," says Captain Brown, "as to the distinctions between the panther and the leopard. Both animals are spotted, and not striped as the tiger is; and the panther is generally allowed to be larger than the leopard, and his range is confined to Africa. Their habits are nearly alike. The panther is capable of domestication, as the following account of an African traveler shows: 'This panther and another were found, when very young, in the forest, apparently deserted by their mother. They were taken to the King of Ashantee, in whose palace they lived several weeks, when my hero, being much larger than his companion, suffocated him in a romping fit, and was sent to Mr. Hutchison at Coomassie. This gentleman, observing that the animal was very docile, took pains to tame him, and in a great measure succeeded.

7. "'Once or twice he stole a fowl, but easily gave it up to his master on being allowed a portion of something else. The day of his arrival he was placed in a small court, and after dinner was led by a thin cord into the room, where he received our salutations with some degree of roughness but with perfect good humor. On the least encouragement he laid his paws upon our shoulders, rubbed his head upon us, and, his teeth and claws having been filed, there was no danger of tearing our clothes.

8. "'He was kept in the above court for a week or two, and showed no ferocity, except when one of the servants tried to pull his food from him. He then caught the offender by the leg and tore out a piece of flesh, but he

never seemed to owe him any ill-will afterward. One morning he broke his cord, and, the cry being given, the castle gates were shut and a chase commenced. After leading his pursuers two or three times around the ramparts, and knocking over a few children by bouncing against them, he suffered himself to be caught and led quietly back to his quarters under one of the guns of the fortress.'"

The Tiger.

9. "While the lion reigns in Africa," writes Hartwig, "the tiger is lord and master of the Indian jungles. A splendid animal, elegantly striped with black on a white and golden ground, graceful in every movement, but of a most bloody and cruel nature. The long body resting on short legs wants the proud bearing of the lion; but the naked head, the rolling eye, the scarlet tongue lolling from the jaws, and the whole expression of the tiger, indicate a blood-thirsty, pitiless ferocity which wreaks itself on every living thing that comes within his grasp. In the bamboo jungle, on the banks of pools and rivers, he waits for the approaching herds. There he seeks his prey, or rather multiplies his murders, for he leaves one victim writhing in the agony of death only to rend and drink the blood of another.

10. "The tiger is particularly fond of dense willow or bamboo bushes on swampy ground, as there he finds the cool shade he requires for his rest during the heat of the day after his nocturnal excursions. It is then very difficult to detect him; but the other inhabitants of the jungle, particularly the peacock and the monkey, betray his presence. The scream of the former is the sure sign that the tiger is rising from his lair; and the monkeys, who during the night are frequently surprised by the panther or the boa, never allow their watchfulness to be at fault during the day. When, on examining a jungle, the traveler sees a monkey quietly seated on the branches, he may be perfectly sure that no dangerous animal lurks about.

The Tiger at Home.

11. "Tiger-hunting is a chief pleasure of the Indian rajahs, who forbid any one else to chase on their domains,

however much their poor vassals may have to suffer in consequence. But the delight they take in tiger-shooting never leads these cautious Nimrods so far as to endanger their precious persons. On some trees of the jungle a scaffolding is prepared at a ludicrous height for his highness, who at the appointed hour makes his appearance with all the pomp of a petty Asiatic despot. The beating now begins, and is executed by a troop of miserable peasants, who most unwillingly submit to this forced and unpaid labor, which is the more dangerous for them, as they are scattered on a long line.

12. "Thus they advance with a dreadful noise of drums, horns, and pistol-firing, driving the wild beasts toward the scaffolding of their lord and master. At first the tigers, startled from their slumbers, retreat before them; but generally, on approaching the scaffolding, they guess the danger that awaits them, and turn with a formidable growl upon the drivers. Nevertheless, great compliments are paid to the noble sportsman who aims a fatal shot from the scaffold, and nobody says a word about the poor, low-born wretches that may have been killed or mutilated by the infuriated brutes."

CHAPTER III.

THE KING OF THE TROPICAL WILDS.

1. "THE majestic form, the noble bearing, the stately stride, the fine proportions, the piercing eye, and the dreadful roar of the lion, striking terror into the heart of every other animal, all combine to mark him with the stamp of royalty. All nerve, all muscle, his enormous

strength shows itself in the tremendous bound with which he rushes upon his prey, in the rapid motions of his tail,

The Lion.

one stroke of which is able to fell the strongest man to the ground, and in the expressive wrinkling of his brow.

2. "The lion is distinguished from all other members of the cat tribe by the uniform color of his tawny skin, by the black tuft at the end of his tail, and particularly by the long and sometimes blackish mane which he is able to bristle when under the influence of passion, and which contributes so much to the beauty of the male, while it is wanting in the lioness, who, as every one knows, is very inferior in size and comeliness to her stately mate.

3. "His chief food consists of the flesh of the larger herbivorous animals, very few of which he is unable to master. Concealed in the high rushes on the river's bank, he lies in ambush for the timorous herd of antelopes which at nightfall approach the water to quench their thirst,

Slowly and cautiously the children of the waste advance. They listen with erect ears, they strain their eyes to pene-

The Lion and its Prey.

trate the thicket's gloom; but nothing suspicious appears or moves along the bank. Long and deeply they quaff the delicious draught, when suddenly, with a giant spring, like lightning bursting from a cloud, the lion bounds upon the unsuspecting revelers, and the leader of the herd lies prostrate at his feet."

4. During the daytime the lion seldom attacks man, and sometimes even when meeting a traveler he is said to pass him by unnoticed; but when the shades of evening descend his mood undergoes a change. After sunset it is dangerous to venture into the woody and wild regions of Mount Atlas, in Africa, for there the lion lies in wait, and there one finds him stretched across the narrow path.

5. It is then that dramatic scenes of exciting interest frequently take place. When, so say the Bedouins, a single man thus meeting a lion is possessed of a brave heart,

he advances toward the monster brandishing his sword or flourishing his rifle high in the air, and, taking good care not to strike or shoot, contents himself with pouring forth a torrent of abuse:

6. "'Oh thou mean-spirited thief!' he says, 'thou pitiful waylayer! thou son of one that never ventured to say no! Think'st thou that I fear thee? Knowest thou whose son I am? Arise and let me pass!' The lion waits till the man approaches quite near him, then he retires, but soon stretches himself once more across the path; and thus by many repeated trials puts the courage of the wanderer to the test. All the time the movements of the lion are attended with a dreadful noise. He breaks numberless branches with his tail; he roars, he growls. Like the cat with the mouse, he plays with the object of his attacks, keeping him perpetually suspended between hope and fear.

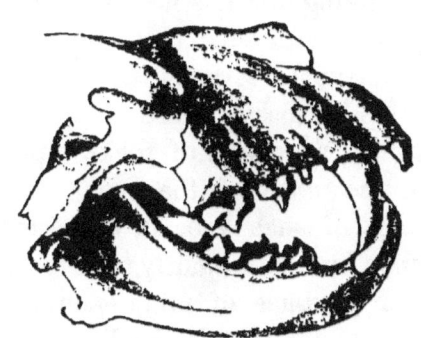

Teeth of the Lion.

7. "If the man engaged in this combat keeps up his courage, if, as the Arabs say, 'he holds fast his soul,' then the brute at last quits him and seeks some other prey; but if the lion perceives that he has to do with an opponent whose courage falters, whose voice trembles, who does not venture a threat,

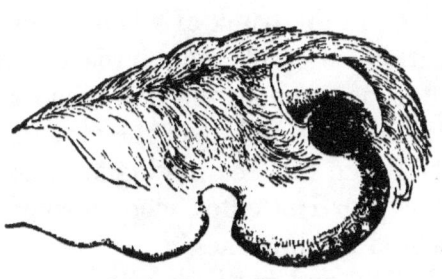

Lion's Claw—Sheathed.

then to terrify him still more he redoubles the performances above described. He approaches his victim, pushes him from the path, then leaves him and approaches him again, and enjoys the agony of the wretch, until at last he tears him to pieces."

Lion's Claw—Unsheathed.

8. The lion is said to have a peculiar liking for the flesh of the Hottentots, and it is surprising with what obstinacy he will follow one of these unfortunate savages. A Hottentot, who endeavored to drive his master's cattle into a pool of water inclosed between two ridges of rocks, espied a huge lion crouching in the midst of the pool. Terrified at the unexpected sight of such a beast, that seemed to have his eyes fixed upon him, he instantly took to his heels. In doing this he had presence of mind enough to run through the herd, concluding that if the lion should pursue he would take the first beast that presented itself.

9. In this, however, he was mistaken. The lion broke through the herd, making directly for the Hottentot, who, on turning round and perceiving that the monster had singled him out, breathless and half dead with fear, scrambled up one of the tree aloes, in the trunk of which a few steps had luckily been cut out to reach some birds' nests on the branches. At the same moment the lion made a spring at him, but, missing his aim, fell upon the ground. In surly silence he walked round the tree, casting at times a dreadful look toward the poor Hottentot, who screened himself from his sight behind the branches.

10. Having remained silent and motionless for a long

time, he at length ventured to peep, hoping that the lion had taken his departure, when, to his great terror and astonishment, his eyes met those of the animal, which, as the poor fellow afterward expressed himself, flashed fire at him. In short, the lion laid himself down at the foot of the tree, and did not move from the place for twenty-four hours. At the end of this time, becoming parched with thirst, he went to a spring at some distance in order to drink. The Hottentot now with great fear ventured to descend, and scampered off home as fast as his feet could carry him.

The Lion at Home.

CHAPTER IV.

THE SULTANA OF THE DESERT.

1. NEAR the close of the last century, while the French army under Bonaparte occupied Egypt, a soldier belonging to the division of Desaix was captured by the Arabs and carried away. In order to put a safe distance between themselves and the French, the Arabs made a forced march through the desert, and at night encamped by a fountain surrounded by palm-trees.

2. Here they bound the hands of their prisoner, fed their horses, made a supper of dates, and all went to sleep. As soon as the Frenchman saw that he was not watched, he unloosed the knot which bound him with his teeth and regained his liberty. He seized a carbine, some dried

The Panther.

dates, and a little bag of grain, and armed with a cimeter he mounted a horse and started off in the direction of the French army.

3. He rode all night and far into the next day, when his weary horse fell down dead and left him alone in the midst of the desert. For a long time he walked on; but at length his strength gave out, and he was obliged to stop. The day was finished; the Oriental night was full

of freshness and beauty. At a little distance he discovered a cluster of palms. To these he dragged his weary limbs, and lay down and slept.

4. He was awakened by the pitiless rays of the sun. The prospect around him filled him with despair. In every direction nothing met his eye but a wide ocean of sand sparkling and glancing in the sunshine. The pure brilliancy of the sky left nothing for the imagination to conceive. Not a cloud obscured its splendor; not a zephyr moved the face of the desert. There was a wild and awful majesty in the universal stillness. God in all his infinite majesty seemed present to the soul.

5. Sad and gloomy the desolate wanderer walked around the little eminence on which the palm-trees grew. To his great joy he discovered on the opposite side a sort of natural grotto, formed in a ledge of granite. Hope was awakened in his breast. Here he might rest in safety. The palms would furnish him with dates for food, and human beings might come that way before they were exhausted.

6. He occupied himself during the day with arranging defenses for the mouth of the grotto, so that he would not be molested by wild beasts, which would probably come in the night-time to drink at the little spring bubbling up at the foot of the palms. Before his fortifications were finished, night came on, and, wearied by his exertions and the extreme heat of the day, he crawled into the grotto and soon fell into a profound sleep.

7. In the night he was awakened by a sudden noise. He started up and listened, and in the deep silence he could hear the loud breathings of some animal. The hair rose upon his head, and he strained his eyes to the utmost to perceive the object of his terror. By the rays of the moon that entered the chinks of the cave, he discovered

an enormous animal lying but a few feet away. There was not sufficient light to distinguish what animal it was. It might be a lion, a tiger, a crocodile; but there was no doubt of the presence of some large and terrible creature.

8. When the moon rose so as to shine directly into the grotto, its beams lighted up the beautiful spotted hide of a huge panther. This lion of Egypt slept with her head upon her paws with the comfortable dignity of a great house-dog. The soldier dared not make the slightest noise lest he should awaken her. Nothing broke the deep silence but the breath of the panther and the strong beatings of his own heart.

9. To attempt her destruction and fail, would be certain death. She was too near to use his carbine. Twice he put his hand upon his cimeter; but the thought of her hard rough skin made him relinquish his project. Day came at last, and showed the jaws of the sleeping panther covered with blood. "She has eaten lately," said the Frenchman to himself; "she will not awake in hunger."

10. She was in truth a beautiful monster. The fur on her throat and legs was a delicate buff; a circle of dark spots like velvet formed bracelets around her paws; her large, muscular tail was buff with rings of black; and the soft, smooth fur of her body was of a glowing yellow, like unwrought gold, richly shaded with dark-brown and black spots. She reposed in the graceful attitude of a puss sleeping on a footstool. Her head rested on her outstretched paws, and her smellers spread out like silver threads.

11. When the sun arose, the panther suddenly opened her eyes, stretched out her paws, and gaped, showing a frightful row of teeth and a great tongue as hard and rough as a file. She then began to wash her paws, pass-

ing them over her ears from time to time as prettily as a kitten. "Very well done," thought the soldier; "she does her toilet very handsomely." He seized a little dagger which he had taken from the Arabs, and prepared to bid her good-morning. At this moment the panther turned her head and saw him.

12. The fixedness of her bright metallic eyes made the soldier tremble. She arose and moved toward him. With great presence of mind he looked her directly in the eye. When she came up to him he gently scratched her head and smoothed her fur. Her eyes gradually softened, and at last she purred like a petted cat; but so deep and strong were her notes of joy that they resounded through the cave like the rolling of a church-organ.

13. The Frenchman redoubled his caresses, and turned and went out of the grotto. The panther came bounding after him, lifting up her back and rubbing like an affectionate kitten. He felt of her ears and throat, and, perceiving that she was pleased with it, he began to tickle the back of her head with the point of his dagger, hoping to find an opportunity to stab her; but her strength and size made him tremble lest he should not succeed.

14. The beautiful sultana of the desert tried the courage of her companion by stretching out her neck and rubbing against him. He raised his arm to give the fatal blow; but at that moment she crouched gently at his feet and looked up in his face with a strange mixture of affection and native fierceness. The soldier's arm fell, and she licked his shoes and purred. During the whole day the panther attended him as a dog does his master, and never suffered him to be out of sight.

15. Taking courage from the past, he began to hope he could get along very comfortably with his new companion. He seated himself by her and patted her neck

until she began again to purr. He took hold of her paws, felt her ears, and rolled her over. She suffered him to do all this; and when he played with her paws she carefully drew in her claws lest she should hurt him. He soon began to have an unwillingness to kill her. In the lonely desert she seemed like a friend. He gave her a name, and before the end of the day she would look up in his face when he called " Mignonne!"

16. When the sun went down she uttered a deep, melancholy cry. "She is well educated," said the soldier; "she has learned to say her prayers!" He was rejoiced to see her grow drowsy. "That is right," said he, "you would better go to sleep first!" When she was sound asleep, he arose silently and set off vigorously toward the Nile; but he had not gone a quarter of a league over the sand when he heard the panther bounding after him, uttering at intervals a loud, sharp cry.

17. Before she came up, the Frenchman fell into a dangerous trap of loose sand, from which he could not extricate himself. The panther seized him by the collar, drew him out of the sand, and brought him safe to the other side of the treacherous ditch at a single bound. "My dear Mignonne," exclaimed the soldier as he caressed her, "our friendship is for life and for death." He retraced his steps. Having hung out his shirt as a signal to any human being who might come near, he lay down and slept.

18. When he awoke, Mignonne was gone. He went out, and soon saw her at a distance clearing the desert with her long and high bounds. She arrived with bloody jaws. When receiving caresses, she purred and fixed her eyes upon him with more fondness than usual. The soldier patted her neck and talked to her as he would to a companion. "Ah, miss, you have been eating some of

the Arabs. Aren't you ashamed? Never mind, they are worse animals than you are; but please don't take a fancy to grind up a poor Frenchman. If you do, you won't have me to love you any more."

19. This animal was so fond of caresses and play, that if her companion sat many minutes without noticing her she would put her paws upon his lap to attract attention. In this way several days passed. The panther became used to the inflections of the soldier's voice and understood the expressions of his face. While her beauty pleased, she delighted him most when she was on a frolic. She showed the perfection of grace and agility as she glided swiftly along, jumping, bounding, and rolling over and over. When she was darting away at full speed, she would stop suddenly when the Frenchman called, "Mignonne!"

20. One day a large bird sailed through the air over their heads. In the desert anything that has life is of interest. The soldier stepped apart to watch the flight of the bird as it slowly and heavily fanned the air. In a few moments the sultana began to growl. "She is certainly jealous," said the soldier, as he looked into her fierce and glittering eyes. They looked at each other, and the proud creature leaped as she felt his hand on her head. Her eyes flashed lightning as she shut them hard. "The creature must have a soul!" exclaimed the Frenchman.

21. This account was given me by the soldier himself as we met near the panther's cage in the menagerie at Paris. "I do not know," continued he, "what I had done to displease Mignonne, or whether the creature was merely in sport; but she turned around, snapped her teeth at me, and seized hold of my leg. Thinking she was about to destroy me, I plunged the dagger into her

neck. The poor creature uttered a cry that froze my very heart. She made no attempt to avenge my blow, but looked mildly upon me in her dying agonies. I would have given all the world to have recalled her to life. It was as if I had murdered a friend. Some French soldiers who saw my signal found me some hours afterward weeping beside her dead body.

22. "Ah, well," said he, after a mournful silence, "I have been in the wars in Germany, Spain, Prussia, and France, but I never had had such sensations as were produced by the lonely desert and my beautiful sultana. In the waste of sand you felt the terrible majesty of God alone. Mignonne came, and with her human sympathies and fears. She died, and the terrible remained. Her mournful cry and the reproachful look of her eyes before they closed in death will haunt me to my dying day."

CHAPTER V.

THE GUARDIANS OF THE HOUSEHOLD.

1. "I think every family should have a dog; it is like having a perpetual baby; it is the plaything and crony of the whole house. It keeps them all young." These words are from that highly cultivated friend of dogs, Dr. John Brown, of Scotland. They express a sentiment which has, to a great extent, been anticipated by the history of that one of all the kingdom of animals that has kept close to man in every part of the globe. Indeed, the friendship of man and his dog is traced back to so remote a period of history, that it can not be certainly determined whether

the family dog is descended from the wolf or the jackal, or whether it is a distinct species.

Faithful and kind.

2. It scarcely needs to be said that the dog is a carnivorous animal, and that his structure is perfectly adapted to secure and dispose of his appropriate food. How many toes the dog has in his fore-paws and hind-paws, and how many teeth he has in his two jaws—how many incisors or cutters, canine or dog teeth, and molars—may be easily ascertained by applying to the dog himself. Among the numerous varieties of dogs, including the most diverse sizes and appearances, there is a unity of feeling. The mastiff and the toy terrier recognize each other as cousins, but neither will take kindly to a tame wolf.

3. Besides the innumerable mixed curs that have no well-defined characteristics, many distinct varieties are our familiar acquaintances. The terrier group embraces the smooth English black-and-tan, the rough Scotch and Isle of Skye, and the fox terriers, all of whom show their inbred propensity to search the *terra* or earth, when the word "rats" is mysteriously pronounced. The spaniel, with soft, curly hair and pendulous ears, is known by his fondness for the water. The mastiff group includes the bull-dog, who makes his attacks without a bark, the famous English mastiff—the prince of watch-dogs—and the abused little pug, whose kingdom is the lap of his mistress. The great, shaggy, noble-hearted Newfoundland is the pride of the household, and the trusted friend of little children.

4. Hundreds of stories have been preserved which illustrate the almost human traits of dogs—their intelligence, reasoning power, memory, humor, jealousy, deceit, sympathy, and fidelity. In ancient Egypt the dog was regarded with veneration. By the Egyptians, Sirius was called the dog-star. But the Eastern nations despised the dog, and from them have descended those phrases and comparisons which class him with objects that are low and wicked.

5. From these people, who never treated this animal as a friend or companion, have come those expressions of anger and insult we too often hear: "You're a dog," "a cur," "a hound." And in the cities and towns of India and Turkey, even to-day, travelers are impressed with what are called "street dogs," who have no masters and no friends.

6. Some gentlemen, who kept tigers in cages, have fed them with the street dogs of India. "I know," says Mr. Williamson, "an instance of one who was thus devoted to

destruction, and was expected to become the tiger's 'daily bread,' standing on the defensive in a manner that completely astonished both the tiger and the spectators. He crept into a corner, and, whenever the tiger approached, seized him by the lip or the nose, making him roar most piteously. The tiger, however, impelled by appetite, for no other supply was given him for several days, would renew the attack. The result was ever the same.

7. "At length the tiger began to treat the dog with more deference, and allowed him not only to eat the mess of rice and meat daily furnished for his subsistence, but even refrained from any attempt to disturb his rest. The two animals, after some weeks, became completely courteous, and each showed symptoms of attachment to his companion. But, what must appear extraordinary, was that the dog, on being allowed free ingress and egress through the hole, considered the cage as his home, always returning to it with confidence, and, when the tiger died, moaning for want of his companion."

8. To illustrate the reasoning power of the dog, John Randolph related the story of one who, in pursuit of his master, came to a place where three roads branched off. The dog scented the ground on the first road, then on the second, and then took the third without using his scent, as much as to say, "He did not go by the first or the second, therefore he must have gone by the third." A Newfoundland dog, annoyed beyond endurance by a small dog, picked the little creature up and dropped it into the water, and afterward rescued it from drowning. Another, whose nose was seized by a bull-dog, who scarcely ever lets go its grip, discovered, near at hand, a kettle of boiling tar. Into this he plunged his tormenter, and received instant relief.

9. Dr. John Brown, of Edinburgh, Scotland, was a

great friend of dogs, and he has written a delightful sketch of his pets, entitled " Rob and his Friends." He gives this graphic account of his dog " Nipper": " Many years ago I got a proof of the unseen and therefore unhelped miseries of the homeless dog. I was walking down Duke Street, when I felt myself gently nipped in the leg. I turned, and there was a ragged little terrier crouching and abasing himself utterly, as if asking pardon for what he had done. He then stood upon end, and begged as only these coaxing little ruffians can.

10. "Being in a hurry, I curtly praised his performance with ' Good dog!' clapped his dirty sides, and, turning round, made down the hill; when presently the same nip—perhaps a little nippier—the same scene, only more intense, the same begging and urgent motioning of his short, shaggy paws. 'There's meaning in this,' said I to myself, and looked at him keenly and differently. He seemed to twig at once, and, with a shrill cry, was off much faster than I could. He stopped every now and then to see that I followed, and, by way of putting off the time and urging me, got up on the aforesaid portion of his body, and when I came up was off again.

11. "This continued till, after going through sundry streets and by-lanes, we came to a gate, under which my short-legged friend disappeared. Of course, I couldn't follow him. This astonished him greatly. He came out to me, and as much as said, ' Why don't you come in?' I tried to open it, but in vain. My friend vanished, and was silent. I was leaving in despair and disgust, when I heard his muffled, ecstatic yelp far off round the end of the wall; and there he was, wild with excitement. I followed, and came to a place where, with a somewhat burglarious ingenuity, I got myself squeezed into a deserted coach-yard, lying all nude and waste.

12. "My peremptory small friend went under a shed, and disappeared in a twinkling through the window of an old coach-body, which had long ago parted from its wheels and become sedentary. I remember the arms of the Fife family were on its panel; and I dare say this chariot with its C-springs had figured in 1822 at the King's visit, when all Scotland was somewhat Fifeish. I looked in, and there was a female pointer with a litter of five pups; the mother like a ghost, and wild with maternity and hunger; her raging, yelling brood tearing away at her dry dugs.

13. "I never saw a more affecting or more miserable scene than that family inside the coach. The poor bewildered mother, I found, had been lost by some sportsman returning south, and must have slunk away there into that deserted place, where she placed her young, rushing out to grab any chance garbage, and running back fiercely to them day after day and night after night.

14. "What the relief was when we got her well fed and cared for, and her children filled and silent, all cuddling about her asleep, and she asleep too, awaking up to assure herself that this was all true, and that there they were, all the five, each as plump as a plum—

> 'All too happy in the treasure
> Of her own exceeding pleasure'—

what this is in kind, and all the greater in amount as many outnumber one, may be the relief, the happiness, the charity experienced and exercised in a homely, well-regulated dog-home.

15. "Nipper, for he was a waif, I took home that night and gave him a name. He lived a merry life with me, showed much pluck and zeal in killing rats, and incontinently slew a cat which had—unnatural brute, un-

like his friend—deserted her kittens and was howling offensively inside his kennel. He died aged sixteen, healthy, lean, and happy to the last. As for Perdita and her pups, they brought large prices, the late Andrew Buchannan, of Coltbridge—an excellent authority and man, the honestest dog-dealer I ever knew—having discovered that their blood and her culture were the best."

CHAPTER VI.

TRAINED AND FAITHFUL SERVANTS.

1. On the top of Mont St. Bernard, in Switzerland, stands a *hospice*, or convent, inhabited by monks, in which for many ages has been preserved a large noble race of dogs specially trained to search for and relieve unfortunate and benighted travelers. The dangers of the mountain-passes, of the deep snows, and of falling avalanches, beset the poor wayfarer, and, if night should overtake him before he reached a human habitation, he often became exhausted, lay down in the snow, and froze to death.

2. On a stormy night these St. Bernard dogs are sent in pursuit of hapless and snow-bound travelers. By their strong scent they are able to find the spot where the victim of misfortune lay, when by their huge paws they clear away the snow, wake the traveler, and by their deep sonorous bark call the monks to the spot, bringing relief. One of these noble dogs won a European reputation, and wore a medal about his neck as a token of distinction, for he had saved the lives of forty persons.

3. The Scotch collie, or shepherd-dog, retains more of the form and appearance of the wolf than any other spe-

cies. In other breeds of dogs the better traits have been found to fade and degenerate; but the excellence of the collie has been so perfectly maintained as to justify the opinion that he is the most perfect of the domestic species. James Hogg, a Scottish shepherd and poet, called the Ettrick Shepherd, says:

4. "Well may the shepherd feel an interest in his dog. He it is indeed that earns the family's bread, of which he is himself content with the smallest morsel, always grateful and always ready to exert his utmost abilities in his master's interest. Neither hunger, fatigue, nor the worst of treatment will drive him from his side. He will follow him through every hardship without murmuring or repining, till he literally falls down dead at his feet."

5. In tending, driving, and guarding sheep, the shepherd-dog discovers an intelligence almost human. He obeys the verbal orders of his master, and his acquaintance with the individuals of a large flock is truly wonderful. Of his faithfulness Scottish writers have recorded numerous instances. Says one: "A shepherd in one of our northern counties had driven part of his flock to a neighboring fair, leaving his dog to watch the remainder during that day and the next night, expecting to see them the following morning.

6. "Unfortunately, however, the shepherd when at the fair forgot his dog and his sheep, and did not reach home till the morning of the third day. His first inquiry was whether the dog had been seen. The answer was 'No.' 'Then,' replied the shepherd with a tone and gesture of anguish, 'he must be dead, for I know he is too faithful to desert his charge.' Instantly he repaired to the heath, when he found the dog just able to crawl. The poor creature crouched to his feet with an expression of joy, and almost immediately expired."

7. The greyhound, the fleetest of foot among all dogs, was a great favorite among the ancient Greeks. His graceful form was in harmony with their refined sentiment of beauty, and his disposition gave him a place in the household and at the family table. He follows his game by sight, though he is not wanting in a delicate sense of smell. The stag or deer hound is the largest and roughest of the hound species. Both his scent and hearing are remarkably acute. Sir Walter Scott held his stag-hound Maida with a fond regard. He was a fine specimen of the breed, and as a consequence was often required to stand for his portrait. This was a keen annoyance, and, the moment he saw a pencil and paper produced, he exhibited intense displeasure.

8. The blood-hound is an affectionate friend and a terrible enemy. Robert Bruce, the hero King of Scotland, cherished his blood-hound with strong affection, and the animal was never happy out of his presence. But Bruce himself was followed by merciless blood-hounds, and on one occasion only escaped death from their blood-thirsty jaws by wading up a brook and so disappointing their scent. Sir William Wallace was saved from a similar death by killing a tired fugitive who accompanied his band. When his English pursuers came upon the dead body, their hounds refused to go farther, the smell of blood overpowering the scent of human tracks.

9. Here is what John Burroughs says of the hound: "The hound is a most interesting dog. How solemn and long-visaged he is! How peaceful and well disposed! He is the Quaker among dogs. All the viciousness and currishness seem to have been weeded out of him; he seldom quarrels, or fights or plays like other dogs. Two strange hounds meeting for the first time behave as civilly toward each other as two men. I know a hound that has

an ancient, wrinkled, human, far-away look that reminds one of the bust of Homer among the Elgin marbles. He looks like the mountains toward which his heart yearns so much.

10. "The hound is a great puzzle to the farm-dog. The latter, attracted by his baying, comes barking and snarling up through the fields, bent on picking a quarrel. He intercepts the hound, snubs and insults and annoys him in every way possible; but the hound heeds him not. If the dog attacks him, he gets away as best he can and goes on with the trail. The cur bristles and barks and struts about for a while, then goes back to the house, evidently thinking the hound a lunatic, which he is for the time being—a monomaniac, the slave and victim of one idea.

11. "I saw the master of a hound one day arrest him in full course, to give one of the hunters time to get to a certain runway. The dog cried and struggled to free himself, and would listen neither to threats nor caresses. Knowing he must be hungry, I offered him my lunch; but he would not touch it. I put it in his mouth; but he threw it contemptuously from him. We coaxed and petted and reassured him; but he was under a spell. He was bereft of all thought or desire but the one passion to pursue that trail."

12. Of the race of hounds, the sleek, smooth pointer, and the silken-haired setter, derived, it is thought, from the pointer and the English spaniel, are the favorites and pets of sportsmen. They are the hunters of ground-birds. Their scent of the peculiar odor which these feathered fugitives leave behind them is remarkable; but the way in which, when they come upon the game sitting, and point it, with the fore-foot raised, as if holding it by the influence of some charm, is something wonderful. And

this tendency to stand over game is an inheritance which is supposed to have descended from the time of the ancient Phœnicians, and is so confirmed that the puppy will take to pointing without any further training than what is necessary to subdue the excess of its spirits.

Esquimau Dogs.

13. In the frigid regions of Asia, Europe, and America, where the sunbeams are too feeble to contend with nightly frost and deep snow, there the dog and the reindeer perform the duties of the horse. The Arctic horse of America is the Esquimau dog. "In this desolate region dogs render invaluable service, not only by drawing sledges, thus transferring persons from place to place, otherwise inaccessible, but enabling them to convey to their dwell-

ings the fish and other animals on which their subsistence depends.

14. "Horses could not be made a substitute for dogs in such countries as these; the severity of the climate and the shortness of the summer render the provision of fodder impossible; the dog alone is adapted to such circumstances, for he can live where other animals would perish, and move quickly over the deep snow in which those heavier than himself would sink. These dogs strongly resemble the wolf. They have long, pointed, projecting noses, sharp and upright ears, and long, bushy tails; some have smooth, while others have curly hair.

15. "They pass the whole time in the open air. In winter they protect themselves by burrowing in the snow; in summer they dig holes in the ground for coolness. Their feeding and training form a particular art, and much skill is required in driving and guiding them. The best-trained dogs are used as leaders; and as the quick and steady going of the team, usually of twelve dogs, and the safety of the traveler, depend on the sagacity of the leaders, no pains are spared so that those intended to go first may always obey their master's voice, and not be tempted from their course by the scent of game."

Esquimau Life.

CHAPTER VII.

"OUR BELOVED BROTHER PRINCE."

1. This brother was a dog. I have never known an instance, except the one here described, in which a quadruped was seriously called brother. But, when you think of it, there is nothing very wrong in the use of this term as it may sometimes be applied. The pug that looks out through the parlor-window, and sits on the same seat with a fashionable lady in her carriage, or is carried in the arms of a dude in the park, is not unworthy to be called brother. And the St. Bernard who digs in Alpine snow and rescues a poor freezing traveler—is not he a brother?

2. It is brother Prince I started to tell about. He was a finely-bred Scotch terrier, and belonged to the Fire Department of St. Louis. Chief Sexton, who has been at the head of the department for many years, is a brave man and has brave men under him. The chief is also a good man, and tender-hearted. He never drinks liquor, and does not allow his men to drink. Both he and his men thought a great deal of Prince. Indeed, Prince was worthy of their esteem, for he was one of the best " boys " in the force.

3. For some time he ran with engine No. 10. Whenever the alarm struck, he jumped from his bed as quickly as if he were charging a rat. He acted the part of a captain or general manager. About the horses, when they were being hitched and started, he ran and dodged, with pattering feet and much uproar, occasionally taking the dangerous risk of biting their heels, until they were under full speed, when he would fall to the rear of the engine, jump on the platform, and ride with the engineer. The

"OUR BELOVED BROTHER PRINCE." 47

men never called him brother, but they treated him like a brother.

4. After a while Prince went to live with the chief. Here he became still more human, and won the name—brother. He always joined the engine or hose-cart when

he knew of the alarm; but he spent the most of his time in the intelligent, joyous sports of the children in the neighborhood. He had a soft, shaggy coat of hair, and the most knowing, playful, roguish pair of eyes.

5. Prince soon became an expert in base-ball. He took his regular place with the other boys in the game, and was obedient to the rules. He was great on "short stops." He would catch a ball in its rapid flight through the air, and before it reached the ground, as well as any other boy. Then he would join the little girls, and be a brother to them, in their games of "hide-and-seek" or "hy-spy," as they call it. Seldom, if ever, was he caught. He always reached the goal or base first.

6. But sometimes—indeed, often for the fun of the thing—he acted as substitute for some unfortunate little one, and became "it." You may be slow to believe it, but I have it on the authority of the chief's daughter, who knew all the freaks and pranks of the dog, when he stood at the base and his companions were seeking hiding-places, he closed one eye, but held the other wide open, and kept perfectly still, waiting for the word "ready." Then he bounced and pranced in all directions, as though there was the smell of rats in the air, until he had disclosed the last hiding-place—himself always reaching the base first.

7. But little Prince, like his playmates, was mortal, and came to a tragic death. On the 10th of August, 1883, about six o'clock in the evening, the alarm sounded at the chief's house, and Prince bounded to the pavement. A hose-carriage whirled around the corner, and he ran to jump on it. The horses were strangers to this little fireman, and one of them kicked him on the head. The great-hearted driver put on his break and stopped the cart, but it was too late. The soulless wheel had passed over his body and he was dead.

8. The hose-carriage passed on. A great crowd of neighbors—men, women, and weeping children—gathered to the scene. "Little Prince is killed!" shouted the ex-

cited children, and in a few minutes the whole neighborhood was on the pavement, while tender little hands bore the body of the dead hero to the chief's house. There were no games in that neighborhood on the 11th of August. It was a day of mourning. Toward sunset nearly a hundred children — white and black — had assembled to bury Prince. In the back yard of the chief's residence was a circular bed covered with flowers of many colors, opening their worshipful faces to heaven. In the middle of this bed a grave was dug. Into a neat little coffin the royal body of Prince was laid.

9. The bearers lowered the coffin into the ground. The grave was filled, and then covered with bouquets of various devices brought by the hands of little mourners bursting with grief. There was a pause and a dead silence. A little colored boy, nine years old, stepped to the head of the grave, while all the boys uncovered their heads, and, with choking voice, made this simple address and prayer: "My beloved brothers and sisters, we are called to de fun'ral of our beloved brother Prince." Then he dropped upon his knees and said: "O Lo'd, our beloved brother Prince was killed last night by de hose-cart, dat run plum ovah him. O Lo'd, we will nevah play with him no mo'. O brothers and sisters, we will meet him in heaven. O Lo'd, save his little soul, shore."

10. A little boy four years old said, "Amen!" There was not a dry eye, and many children sobbed aloud. They sang a familiar Sunday-school hymn, and silently, solemnly parted. A strange brotherhood!—children, white and black, and a dead dog. But—

"One touch of nature makes the whole world kin."

CHAPTER VIII.

SAVAGE DOGS OF FOREST AND PLAIN.

1. THE story of Little Red Riding Hood has made the wolf a familiar name. Rarely if ever are wolves seen by people in the old settled communities of America, and we depend for our knowledge of them upon the narratives of

The Wolf.

the early settlers and woodsmen, about whose cabins at night the howl of the prowling wolf was not uncommon. The wolf belongs to the dog family, and in structure is precisely like the dog. The American wolf is gray, with long, coarse hair, bushy tail, and is from three to four feet long. The European wolf is more tawny in color, but in other respects is not essentially different.

2. Closely allied to the wolf is the jackal, who inhabits the wilds of Asia and Africa. He is between the wolf and the fox in size, and, when tamed, shows more of the disposition of the domestic dog. Hence, some have sup-

posed the jackal to be the original parent of the dog. On our far Western plains, and about the Rocky Mountains, abounds the prairie-wolf, or coyote, about the size of the jackal. He is timid and harmless to man, though he loves to prowl about the settlement and camp, and act the part of a sly thief. The wolf has a more continuous howl, but the coyote is known by a snapping bark; and the noise of a single individual sounds to the stranger like the barking of a numerous pack.

The Coyote.

3. "In those plains of Siberia that are infested by wolves, a sledge-journey is far from agreeable, for frequently a band of these ferocious brutes persistently follow travelers. If the sledge stops for only a second, the men and horses are lost; safety exists only in flight. The struggle on such occasions is fearful. The horses, mad with terror, seem to have wings. The wolves follow on their track, their eyes flashing with fire. It is a terrible situation to be placed in, to behold these black specters tearing across the surface of the white shroud of snow, thirsting for blood. From time to time a report is heard—a wolf falls.

4. "More audacious than the others, the victim had tried to climb the sledge, and one of the travelers had shot it. This incident gives some advantage to the fugitives; for the carnivorous troop halt for a few seconds to devour the body of their companion. But the end is nigh; the village or castle appears against the gray sky, and the

wolves are deprived of their anticipated prey. At other times the adventure terminates in a tragical manner. After the pursuit of some hours, the team, exhausted and incapable of proceeding farther, is overtaken; the sledge is surrounded and carried by assault; the rest may be imagined!"

5. "In 1739, Israel Putnam, who afterward became so well known as General Putnam, of the Revolutionary War, began life as a farmer in the town of Pomfret, Connecticut, forty miles east of Hartford. That part of the State was then quite wild, and the wolves were so troublesome that they killed seventy of his sheep in one night. The mischief was all done by one old she-wolf and her cubs, who had lived in the woods near there for several years. The hunters killed the cubs, but the old one was too wary to be caught. She was at last driven by bloodhounds into a den about three miles from Putnam's house.

6. "The hunters tried to smoke her out by burning straw and brimstone in the mouth of the cave, but the wolf would not come out, and Putnam, tired of waiting any longer, for it was then ten o'clock at night, took a blazing torch in his hand and went down the hole, which was only high enough for him to crawl on his hands and knees. He had a rope tied round his legs, and told his friends to pull him up when he gave the signal.

7. "He crawled along more than thirty feet without seeing anything; but all at once he saw at the end of the cave the glaring eyeballs of the wolf. She gnashed her teeth and gave a sudden growl, and his friends, who heard it, pulled him out so quickly that his shirt was torn to strips and his skin badly cut.

8. "He then loaded his gun with buck-shot, and, taking it in one hand and a torch in the other, went down again. As soon as he came near the wolf she growled and

made ready to spring on him, but he shot her quickly in the head, and was hauled out again, nearly deaf with the noise, and choked with the smoke. After the smoke had cleared away, he crawled down a third time, took the dead wolf by the ears, and the two were pulled out by the people above with much joy.

9. "When the wolves get into the habit of visiting a particular neighborhood, they continue the practice for several nights almost consecutively, and the farmers there become very vigilant, getting all animals safely housed before dark. The wolf comes into the farm-yard, and the creatures in the buildings know that he is there, and pass wakeful and anxious hours. One night in winter, when there were wolves about the farm I live on, I went, about midnight, to the stable, and, just on coming out, I met a fine wolf face to face. We were not more than six or eight feet from each other, and both rather taken by surprise. I had no weapon, but remembered the tradition that you must never turn your back upon a wolf, so I stood still and asked him what he wanted.

10. "The sound of a human voice seems to have affected the wolf's mind, for he turned round and slinked away into the dark shades of a neighboring wood. The morning after, I learned that he had killed a goat on the next farm. I exactly remember what passed in my mind during our brief meeting: 'That's a large dog; no, it is not a dog, it is something else; what else?—wolf—no weapon —must keep my face to him.' Then, aloud, 'Well, sir, what do you want here?' On which he looked steadfastly at me for a second or two without stirring, then made a rapid right-about-face, and cantered woodward in perfect silence."

COYOTE.

1. Blown out of the prairie in twilight and dew,·
   Half bold and half timid, yet lazy all through;
   Loath even to leave, and yet fearful to stay,
   He limps in the clearing, an outcast in gray.

2. A shade on the stubble, a ghost on the wall,
   Now leaping, now limping, now risking a fall,
   Lop-eared, and large-jointed, but ever alway
   A thoroughly vagabond outcast in gray.

3. Here, Carlo, old fellow—he's one of your kind—
   Go, seek him, and bring him in out of the wind.
   What! snarling, my Carlo? So—even dogs may
   Deny their own kin in the outcast in gray.

4. Well, take what you will—though it be on the sly,
   Marauding or begging—I shall not ask why;
   But will call it a dole, just to help on his way
   A four-footed friar in orders of gray!

Bret Harte.

CHAPTER IX.

SLY-BOOTS.

1. THE shower is passing, the woods are shaking the warm rain-drops from their summits, and from the heath a refreshing and spicy fragrance rises through the evening air. In every retreat feet and wings are on the move. The gnats begin their dance, the ants creep forth to repair their flooded highway, the chaffinch is warbling from the top of the beech-tree, the hare is at her play, and the Fox begins to feel his nature stir within him.

Making his Choice.

2. He is on the watch, yonder, between the roots of an old oak; he scents something. There is nothing to fear. All Nature, drunken with the influence of spring, is reveling in the balmy air. With a single bound Reynard is at the threshold. Now you can see him distinctly. How he stands there! With what a high-bred air, and how conscious of his own importance! You see at a glance that noble blood rolls in his veins. He has an air about him at once of dignity and daring. With such a character, it is worth while to observe both him and his dress somewhat closely.

3. His forehead is low, the skin tightly drawn over it, craft lurking in its very smoothness. The ear, sharply pointed at the extremity, widens at the base to catch every passing sound. It is made for obtaining the faintest trace of the prey sleeping in the trees above; the slightest noise—the trembling of a leaf, the quiver of a dreaming bird—falls into the listening aperture; nothing escapes him. And then the nose! How much malice and grace, how much spirit, lies in that fine long, stretched-out, supple point! Does it not seem as if a thousand invisible feelers issued thence, and that here, as its central point, is the very soul of all this contriving and treachery?

4. But the most interesting face is nothing if we forget the eyes. It is true, the fox's eye can not be termed beautiful. You recognize in it, at once, the mighty instinct of prey: its color plays between a gray and green; it lies askant, half hidden in the cavity, and by day drawn together into a mere perpendicular chink. Now it is lowered in humble resignation, or it gazes around in simplicity and innocence; now a derisive smile plays about the lids, and then again a look is darted forth, keen and venomous, as though you had been struck suddenly by the fangs of a viper.

5. All the other parts of the body are in harmony with the face. The mouth stretches wide, for the fox kills its prey; a spare beard is ranged around the upper lip, in long, receding points; those lips, too, are finely cut and closed; they indicate energy and self-command. But, if they move apart, the sharp, white teeth glisten fiercely; or, gnashing with rage, a hoarse, cough-like, snapping bark is heard. Swift feet carry the slender, hanging body, with its bushy train, almost trackless over the ground. On his breast he wears a delicate white shirt-front, and his fur gleams red and golden.

6. Thus formed and clad and furnished, the cunning one goes creeping, slinking, and winking through life; he wends and bends, is cautious, persevering, agile, and ever resolute; the master of a hundred arts, whom one can not help admiring and hating in the same breath.

7. But to return to our fox, still leaning against his door-post. Soon two or three young foxes make their appearance; and now, as the mother steps out of her dwelling, the old fox departs to obtain his family supplies. With his tail dragging after him, he silently creeps through bush and field, and always in a slanting direction. He soon reaches the park where the roe grazes undisturbed by man. He creeps along ever more slowly and softly.

8. The evening breathes coolly from every stem and leaf. The summits of the trees rise motionless in the silence; the throats of the birds alone are still heard. The thrush is warbling in clear tones; the titmouse, chirping its pert little song, passes from bush to bush; the carpenter woodpecker is chopping and hammering at an old oak-stump; the jay's noisy screech is heard now and then, with a strange, jeering flourish; and when again all is quite still, from the depths of the green solitude there comes the mournful cry of the pewit.

9. Reynard has reached the border of the glade; he listens. A crackling is heard among the branches; a low whistle is audible. A roe steps forth, her head raised on high, and her eyes turned in every direction. Another whistle, and with graceful bounds the fawn is at its mother's side. With droll and pretty gambols it plays around her. The mother licks its neck lovingly. But presently the roe lifts her head. She has got wind of the robber. Her eyes sparkle, and she makes a bound or two, her hoofs making unpleasant music in the ears that rise above that hungry mouth.

10. But Reynard does not lose heart. He stands still for a moment, and then vanishes. He makes a wide circle and comes around on the other side. The fawn is ever in his eye. Now he is within convenient distance, he crouches down like a cat; his eyes stare with fierce greediness; he shows his murderous fangs; and, as he gathers himself for the last fatal spring—a bound, and the watchful mother rushes on the robber and tramples him with her feet. The fawn is saved. Reynard turns home sore and lame, and burning with rage. The next time, we fear, he may have better luck.

11. When brown autumn comes on, then is the golden time for the fox. A ripening calm is spread over the earth; the ears of corn hang down, heavy and yellow, an endless wood of fruit. Hares and rabbits are crouched there; partridges, quails, and larks; little people without arms or defense, who lead a harmless and industrious life. Ah! it will fare ill with them now. He, the crafty one, enters the field. He can wait and bait, can cower and devour, and knows how, with guile and wile, to scare and ensnare. Their little arts are all in vain; and his cubs, as they grow older, get fatter and bolder.

12. When his hunger is satisfied, the bee-hive attracts

him. He springs up and laps the sweet drops, even though the whole swarm buzz around him in their fury; he laughs at their sting, and, receiving them on his fur, rolls himself on the ground, crushes and eats them; so at last the busy workers are obliged to resign to him the sweet store, and desert their house and home. Or he steals into the vineyard to taste the grapes, if not too high or too sour; or he lies in ambush near the brook to go halves with the heron in her prey, or to tickle the crayfish with his brush, and coax him out of his watery cave.

13. But cold winter approaches. The migratory birds are off to the land of the sun. The few of the feathered tribes that remain roost high on the trees. He looks at them wistfully, but makes no vain attempt to disturb their repose. The hare sits securely in his form in the distant field, and the rabbit lies snug in his chambers under-ground. Now the farm-yard allures, and happy is the fox if, at night, some unguarded hole allows him to enter the house

The Fox in Luck.

where hens and chickens repose in fancied security. He discovers his prey, and makes a frantic leap, but misses.

He gnashes his teeth, leaps up again and again, more passionate, more greedy, and at last, with a mighty bound, he seizes his victim and darts away to his home among the rocks.

14. But farm-yards are not always open, and the keen demands of appetite increase from day to day. The distant bay of the watch-dog warns him away from the village. He roams through the woods with the gloomiest thoughts. On a sudden he raises his nose, his eyes flash, a sweet savor is borne gently toward him. Ha! what is this? Behold, in the midst of the hungry wood, a delicious morsel of roast rabbit! He snatches and swallows it in an instant. His vital powers are renewed, his eyes grow fresher, and with senses sharpened he trots forward. And verily there lies a second morsel! It is no fancy; it is of the same savor, the same flesh and bone. Reynard pauses. His suspicions are aroused. With shy steps he creeps around the spot, again pauses, crouches down, listens. There is not a sound, save the grating of the old fir-trees. He springs forward, and the second piece is swallowed.

15. Again he starts onward, licking his chops over the dainty which has served to but whet his appetite—and there, full before him, is the third morsel. The smell is cruel to the poor hungry creature, and from a distance he devours the bait with his eyes. But this time he is more cautious. He moves around the dainty food in circles. Again he cowers, lays his ears forward, backward, pricks them up, and makes sure that it is safe on every hand. Again all is mute, the firs alone grate on in a surly way. It is as if Nature held her breath. But the delicious scent takes full possession of him. He must approach. With one wild bound he leaps, when—crack!—the iron jaws of the trap clash their teeth together. He howls with pain

and rage, but his leg is held fast. But death is in delay. A bold deed is called for.

> "His leg is caught by the iron grim;
> To save his life he yields his limb,
> And off he gnaws it, though great the smart;
> He has a bold, courageous heart!"

Away he goes, bounding as if he had only pulled off a boot, and he is a wary old fox as long as he lives.

Masius.

CHAPTER X.

SLYER THAN A FOX.

1. Fox-hunting is a popular sport in the Conhocton Valley, Steuben County, New York, and in the past foxes seem to have been plenty. The most successful hunter of

The Fox at Home.

foxes in the region is William Kelsey, of Avoca. When the skins of foxes commanded a high price in the market a few years ago, these animals were hunted and trapped for profit, and hundreds were shipped to market during the months in which the fur was valuable. Then it was that Kelsey distinguished himself by daily bringing in from three to ten foxes, while other famed hunters and trappers frequently returned from the chase empty-handed.

2. Kelsey would permit no one to hunt in his company, or go with him when setting his traps. He accumulated a fair fortune by his success in getting skins. His brother hunters were extremely jealous of his success. Some of them believed that he was possessed of a secret by which he charmed foxes to his traps and within range and reach of his gun.

3. "There's more ways than one to get the best of a fox," said Kelsey, recently; "you want to be observant of their nature, in the first place. In the second place, you want to be just as sly and cunning as they are. When I used to hunt foxes for profit, I don't mind saying now, I had three favorite ways of killing them. When I was a boy, I was hunting a fox with a hound. During the chase the hound went lame in one of his legs. He was a blooded dog and full of game, and kept right on after the fox; but he ran slower, of course. It wasn't long before I noticed a difference in that fox's running.

4. "He actually seemed to take delight in not attempting to elude the dog by cunning, but in keeping just far enough ahead to be in sight and hearing of him, as if to tantalize him. The fox, of course, intended, after having his little fun with the lame dog, at last to summon his cunning to his aid and get out of the way to a place of safety. After noticing the unmistakable behavior of the fox, it was easy for me to get a position where a shot at him was certain, whereas if the dog had been able-bodied the fox would have been twisting and turning in all sorts

of ways miles away, and at last probably would have succeeded in getting away. I tried this lame hound another day. He started a fox which, as soon as he saw the dog was lame, adopted the same tactics as the other one had.

5. "That settled in my mind that if a fox only felt certain of eventually getting a safe hiding-place, being chased by a hound was just as much fun for him as it was for the hunter, and he would enjoy it just so long as he felt inclined to. I have hunted foxes with a hound disabled in one leg ever since, and never found one fox yet that wouldn't take things most tantalizingly easy with the dog, and never failed to get every fox I started, unless my gun went back on me.

6. "I found also that foxes were inordinately fond of field-mice. There were some places where field-mice were quite plenty, but as a general thing they were scarce. So I trapped a number of them and went to breeding them. They were very prolific, and I soon had a wide extent of country stocked with mice. I selected old fields, on the edge of woods or brush-lots. The foxes were not long in finding out where the mice were thickest. They generally came to feed on them just between sunset and dark, when the mice were out in force, squeaking and playing about. You could hear them squeak about the fields plainly, and I noticed that a fox would enter a field and listen for the noise. As soon as he heard a mouse squeak, he would steal up as a fox only can, and that mouse was his.

7. "Hidden behind a convenient bush, it was no trouble for me to gather in sometimes three or four foxes in an evening. Watching the foxes in the fields answering the squeal of a mouse, I concluded I could improve on my plan of hunting. I made a whistle that I could blow on and exactly imitate the noise made by a field mouse. By

this I could call a fox toward me if the mice were not near me, and I got a great many shots that I otherwise would not have had; and, of course, every time I had a shot it meant another fox added to my list. The whistle not only drew foxes to me that were in the field, but it brought them into the field, for a fox can hear a mouse's squeal for a long distance.

8. "I used to have great sport hunting foxes in another way, peculiarly my own. My observations of the habit of foxes led to the discovery that, early in the fall and winter mornings, they sought wood-lots where fire had been through, and where many charred stumps and trunks of trees were standing. I have seen as many as ten foxes in a group in a lot of this kind, but they generally were seen trotting leisurely along among the blackened stumps, stopping now and then to look cautiously about. I never could find out why foxes sought this place; but I never failed to find at least one in any lot I visited. I noticed another peculiarity about foxes when I studied them among these burned trees. A fox would trot along for probably ten rods, when suddenly he would give a little kick or twitch with one hind-leg, stop, and invariably turn his head and look back over his shoulder. I observed this at different times in different foxes, and concluded that it was a natural characteristic of the species.

9. "I determined to make this little piece of knowledge result in adding to my list of successes in fox-hunting. Although I saw so many foxes in burned wood-lots, it was seldom that I could get a shot at any of them, as they were so cautious, and to get within shooting distance was impossible. The shots I did get were the result of accident, a fox now and then coming toward where I hid. So I hit upon a plan that would be systematic, and, I

thought, successful in capturing foxes. I dressed in black clothes from head to foot, and blackened my face and hands. There was nothing to be seen about me but black. When I took my position one morning among the blackened stumps and trunks of a burned wood-lot, I looked enough like them to deceive the sharpest eye. With my gun ready I stood motionless.

10. "Presently I saw a fox trotting along in the opposite direction, and I started after it, keeping my eyes fastened upon it. When I saw the leg twitch I became motionless. When the fox took his look backward, I was as good a burned tree as there was in the lot. The fox saw nothing to cause him any fear, and on he went. Before he gave the warning twitch again I was a great deal closer to him than I was before. My *ruse* was still undiscovered by him, and the third time he kicked his hind-leg he never looked back, for I was within easy gun-shot and saved him the trouble. My new style of hunting foxes succeeded so well, and it required such a nice eye and such careful calculation, that it became my favorite sport and afforded me a great deal of amusement.

11. "As to trapping foxes, a little common sense used in a simple manner was the entire secret of my great success. It was the usual custom in setting a fox-trap to place the bait on the trap. A fox is always suspicious. When he sees a piece of meat or a dead bird, chicken, or whatever it may be, lying near or in the barn-yard, or wherever the trap may be set, he does not make a dash for it at once. He feels that there is something wrong; yet his curiosity and his desire for the tempting morsel will lead him to investigate the matter. Many and many a sly old fox has conquered his appetite and his curiosity on close inspection of a bait of this kind, and placed as much distance as he could between himself and the dangerous

place; but now and then one will venture to seize the bait and get caught.

12. "A fox's manner of approaching a baited trap is peculiar. He trots around in circles, beginning with large ones, and gradually narrowing them until he reaches the bait, upon which he keeps constantly his suspicious but greedy eye. After watching an old fox approach a trap in this way, and get near enough to seize the bait, and then seeing him turn and get away from the spot as fast as he could, I concluded that I knew a trick worth two of his. I placed my bait on the ground and set my trap, nicely hidden from view, several feet away. When the fox came and began his circling around, with his eyes constantly on the meat he coveted, the first thing he knew he stepped on the hidden trap, and he was no longer interested in the bait that tempted him. I never knew this manner of setting a fox-trap to fail in capturing the fox if one came to inspect the bait where it was set."

CHAPTER XI.

PESTS OF THE HOUSEHOLD.

"When I was a bachelor I lived by myself,
   And all the bread and cheese I had I laid upon a shelf;
   But the rats and the mice they made such a strife,
   I was forced to go to London to buy me a wife."

1. So we learn from Mother Goose herself that even in the golden age of childhood the bread and cheese suffered from nibbling the same as now, and that, probably as now, sleepers in the night then were disturbed by gnawings in the cupboard, or by the soft pattering of

nimble little feet across the floor. Indeed, we may say that houses are built for men and mice: they go in together, they live together; and not until the last human occupant departs do the gnawings and squeakings cease.

2. The rat and the mouse are rodents, animals made for gnawing, and gnaw they must. The nose of a rat is pointed, and in the front part of each jaw are two chisel-like teeth. On examining them we find that the inner part is of an ivory-like substance, which is easily worn away, while the outside is composed of a glass-like enamel, which is excessively hard. The upper teeth work exactly into the under, in the act of gnawing, so that the soft part is continually worn away, while the hard part keeps a sharp, chisel-like edge. At the same time the teeth grow up from the bottom, so that as they wear away they are continually renewed.

3. In consequence of this arrangement, if one of the teeth be removed or accidentally broken, the opposite tooth will continue to grow, until it will project from the mouth and cease to be of any use. Rats have been killed with an upper tooth grown long and bent into a complete circle, or with an under tooth piercing the skull above. The ceaseless gnawings are thus seen to be a necessity, for, if the rat did not gnaw for a living, he would be obliged to gnaw to prevent his teeth from growing so as to fill his mouth and render his jaws useless.

4. These pests of the household live in the hollow spaces in the walls, in burrows opening from the cellar-bottoms, in drains, and in all sorts of out-of-the-way holes and crevices. Wherever there is a place for a rat there is a rat to occupy it. Both rats and mice increase with such fearful rapidity that if they were not kept down they would soon overrun a house and render it uninhabitable by human beings. It is estimated that a pair of

rats if undisturbed for three years would increase to more than 650,000!

Rats feeding.

5. Every man's hand and foot is against a rat: little dogs bark at the sound of his squeal, little boys shout when he is caught; little girls hold him in fear equal to that of the rattlesnake; and young ladies climb chairs at mention of his name. Traps, dogs, cats, ferrets, poison, are all used to rid the world of him; and yet he keeps his place in the household, nibbles the rich man's cheese, the farmer's corn, the sailor's biscuit, forces his way into palace and hovel, and shares alike the rice of the Hindoo and the winter stores of the Norwegian.

6. In cities the rat communities vastly outnumber the human population. Their streets are the underground sewers, and through these they pass securely from one part of the city to another. From them they enter cellars

and attics, and become members of every household. They find a living in the contents of the sewers, and they feed upon the garbage which is left in neglected corners. They prefer a frugal diet where there is no fear of enemies; but when driven by hunger they courageously face great danger to get at the supplies of the family. While destroying much that is valuable, they also do a beneficent work as scavengers. From their place in the drains they devour every morsel of concentrated fever and cholera as it comes down to them, so preserving their own lives, and saving the lives of little children playing above.

7. Then the rat is one of the most cleanly animals in his personal habits. No matter how filthy the streets he traverses, no matter how foul the air he breathes, or the food he eats, he allows no soil upon his person. When we see a rat at rest, he is always cleaning himself. Frank Buckland says, "Never does a rat finish a bit of food, or is touched by a human hand, but that he cleans himself immediately afterward."

8. In London and Paris rat-catching is a regular profession. The rat-catchers, with lantern and bag, enter the larger sewers and pursue the rats into some blind alley, and then, when there is no chance for escape, they are seized and bagged. The hand of the rat-catcher must be protected by a thick leather glove. When driven to bay, the rats will make a ferocious attack upon the man, when nothing but the thickness of his long boots will preserve his life.

9. In country places, when rats congregate in great numbers, they become an intolerable scourge. Impelled by hunger, they eat the crops of the farmer, and when they have devoured the contents of one barn they migrate to another. They often may be seen pursuing a direct course toward the mow of unthrashed grains, and all

moving together. But the curious thing is, how do they know where to go? Did they send out scouts, or does instinct guide them?

10. Bermuda was settled in 1614. With the first settlers came the rats. Two years later they had increased at such a rate that they had become a general scourge. They had nests in every tree, and they burrowed in the ground like rabbits. They devoured everything that came in their way, fruits, plants, and even trees. When corn was sown, they would come by troops in the night and scratch it from the ground.

11. A writer of the time says, "They so devoured the fruits of the earth that the people were destitute of bread for a year or two." Every expedient was tried to destroy them. Dogs were trained to hunt them, who would kill a score or two in an hour. Cats, both wild and tame, were employed for the same purpose. Poisons were employed, and every man was enjoined by law to set twelve traps. Even woods were set on fire to help exterminate them. "Rats are a great judgment of God upon us," wrote a colonist in 1617. "At last it pleased God, by what means it is not well known, to take them away, insomuch that the wild cats and many dogs that lived upon them famished."

12. A telegraph inspector of England made good use of a rat to help him out of a difficulty. It was necessary to overhaul a cable of wires inclosed in iron tubes. A length of the cable had been taken out of the tube, without the precaution of attaching a wire by which it might be drawn back. When the repairs were made, the question arose, how the cable could be again drawn into the tube. After due reflection the inspector invoked the aid of a rat-catcher, and, provided with a large rat, a ferret, and a ball of string, they repaired to the scene of action.

13. The "flush-boxes" were opened, and the rat, with an end of the string attached to his body, was put into the pipe. He scampered away at a racing pace, dragging the twine after him, until he reached the middle of the length of pipe, and there stopped. The ferret was then put in, and off went the rat again, until he sprang clear out of the next flush-box. One half of the work was done, and the same operation was commenced with the next length of pipe, but the rat stopped short a few yards in the pipe, and boldly awaited the approach of the ferret. A sharp combat began, and it was feared that one or both the animals would die in the pipe. But, after sundry jerks of the string, the combatants separated; the ferret returned to his master, and the rat made for the extremity, carrying the string through in safety.

14. Rats are often tamed, and make pretty household pets. They are clean, playful, and, when well fed, harmless. In Belgium, not long since, a troop of rats were trained to perform a play. They were dressed in the garb of men and women, walked on their hind-legs, and went through with great exactness the ordinary stage actions. On one point, however, they were like the cat who had been changed to a young lady, but forgot her own character the moment a mouse appeared. When, in the course of the play, food was introduced, they forgot their parts, the audience, and the manager, and, dropping on all-fours, they fell to with all the native voracity of their race. The performance concluded by their hanging in triumph their enemy the cat, and dancing around her body.

15. Many are the expedients to get rid of rats. Holes are smeared with tar, which rats can not abide. Singed rats are set at liberty and sent to drive away the others by their scent. A tiny bell is placed on the neck of a rat, and he thereafter in vain tries to associate with his race;

they all fly at his approach. A farmer rid himself of rats by the following simple device: He had a granary rat-proof, but he purposely left one hole where rats might go in and out. After they became accustomed to the route, great numbers would congregate, but run out of the hole the moment the door was open. Waiting one time until the army of rats were well at work, he slipped a bag over the hole on the outside, when he opened the door. The rats scampered, as usual, and were all bagged at once. In the "Pied Piper of Hamelin," we have another novel way of rat-extermination, together with a rat-commentary upon it:

16. " Into the street the Piper stept,
　　　Smiling first a little smile,
　　As if he knew what magic slept
　　　In his quiet pipe the while;
　　Then, like a musical adept,
　　To blow the pipe his lips he wrinkled,
　　And green and blue his sharp eyes twinkled,
　　Like a candle-flame where salt is sprinkled;
　　And ere three shrill notes he uttered,
　　You heard as if an army muttered;
　　And the muttering grew to a grumbling;
　　And the grumbling grew to a mighty rumbling;
　　And out of the houses the rats came tumbling—
　　Great rats, small rats, lean rats, brawny rats,
　　Brown rats, black rats, gray rats, tawny rats,
　　Grave old plodders, gay young friskers,
　　　Fathers, mothers, uncles, cousins,
　　Cocking tails and pricking whiskers,
　　　Families by tens and dozens;
　　Brothers, sisters, husbands, wives—
　　Followed the Piper for their lives.

From street to street he piped advancing,
And step by step they followed dancing,
Until they came to the river Weser,
   Wherein all plunged and perished.

17. "Save one, who, stout as Julius Cæsar,
   Swam across, and lived to carry
     (As he the manuscript he cherished)
To Rat-land home his commentary,
Which was, 'At the first shrill notes of the pipe,
I heard a sound as of scraping tripe,
And putting apples wondrous ripe
Into a cider-press's gripe;
And a moving away of pickle-tub boards,
And a leaving ajar of conserve-cupboards,
And a drawing the corks of train-oil flasks,
And a breaking the hoops of butter-casks;
And it seemed as if a voice
   (Sweeter far than by harp or by psaltery
Is breathed) called out: 'O rats, rejoice!
   The world has grown to one vast dry-saltery!
So munch on, crunch on, take your nuncheon,
Breakfast, supper, dinner, luncheon!'
And just as a bulky sugar-puncheon,
Already staved, like a great sun, shone
Glorious; scarce an inch before me,
   Just as methought it said, 'Come, bore me!'
—I found the Weser rolling o'er me!'"

CHAPTER XII.

THE LEGEND OF BISHOP HATTO.

Near Bingen on the Rhine is an old tower, known as the "Rat-Tower" of Bishop Hatto. The tower is shown in the engraving. It is said to be more than a thousand years old. The old German legend concerning it is well told in the following poem:

1. The summer and autumn had been so wet,
That in winter the corn was growing yet;
'Twas a piteous sight to see, all around,
The grain lie rotting on the ground.

2. Every day the starving poor
Crowded around Bishop Hatto's door,
For he had a plentiful last-year's store;
And all the neighborhood could tell
His granaries were furnished well.

3. At last Bishop Hatto appointed a day
To quiet the poor without delay;
He bade them to his great barn repair,
And they should have food for the winter there.

4. Rejoiced such tidings good to hear,
The poor folk flocked from far and near;
The great barn was full as it could hold
Of women and children, and young and old.

5. Then when he saw it could hold no more,
Bishop Hatto he made fast the door;
And while for mercy on Christ they call,
He set fire to the barn and burnt them all.

6. "I' faith, 'tis an excellent bonfire!" quoth he,
"And the country is greatly obliged to me,

THE LEGEND OF BISHOP HATTO.

For ridding it in these times forlorn
Of rats that only consume the corn."

The Rat-Tower at Bingen on the Rhine.

7. So then to his palace returnèd he,
   And he sat down to supper merrily;
   And he slept that night like an innocent man,
   But Bishop Hatto never slept again.

8. In the morning, as he entered the hall
   Where his picture hung against the wall,

  A sweat like death all over him came,
  For the rats had eaten it out of the frame.

9. As he looked, there came a man from his farm;
  He had a countenance white with alarm:
  "My lord, I opened your granaries this morn,
  And the rats had eaten all your corn."

10. Another came running presently,
  And he was as pale as pale could be—
  "Fly! my lord bishop, fly," quoth he,
  "Ten thousand rats are coming this way—
  The Lord forgive you for yesterday!"

11. "I'll go to my tower on the Rhine," replied he,
  "'Tis the safest place in Germany;
  The walls are high, and the shores are steep,
  And the stream is strong, and the water deep."

12. Bishop Hatto fearfully hastened away,
  And he crossed the Rhine without delay,
  And reached his tower, and barred with care
  All the windows, doors, and loop-holes there.

13. He laid him down and closed his eyes;
  But soon a scream made him arise;
  He started, and saw two eyes of flame
  On his pillow, from whence the screaming came.

14. He listened, and looked—it was only the cat,
  But the bishop grew more fearful for that;
  For she sat screaming, mad with fear
  At the army of rats that were drawing near.

15. For they have swum over the river so deep,
  And they have climbed the shores so steep,

And up the tower their way is bent,
To do the work for which they were sent.

16. They are not to be told by the dozen or score;
By thousands they come, and by myriads, and more.
Such numbers had never been heard of before;
Such a judgment had never been witnessed of yore.

17. Down on his knees the bishop fell,
And faster and faster his beads did he tell,
As louder and louder, drawing near,
The gnawing of their teeth he could hear.

18. And in at the windows, and in at the door,
And through the walls, helter-skelter they pour,
And down from the ceiling, and up through the floor,
From the right and the left, from behind and before,
From within and without, from above and below,
And all at once to the bishop they go.

19. They have whetted their teeth against the stones;
And now they pick the bishop's bones;
They gnawed the flesh from every limb,
For they were sent to do judgment on him!

Robert Southey.

CHAPTER XIII.

NUT-CRACKERS AND WOOD-CUTTERS.

" The mountain and the squirrel
    Had a quarrel;
And the former called the latter ' Little prig.'
    Bun replied,
' You are doubtless very big;

> But all sorts of things and weather
> Must be taken in together,
> To make up a year
> And a sphere,
> And I think it no disgrace
> To occupy my place.
> If I'm not so large as you,
> You are not so small as I,
> And not half so spry.
> I'll not deny you make
> A very pretty squirrel-track;
> Talents differ; all is well and wisely put;
> If I can not carry forests on my back,
> Neither can you crack a nut.'"

1. The rat is not without kindred near at home. Besides the mice, it has a rodent cousin in the trees, with the same bright eyes, gnawing teeth, and quick motions. This is the squirrel, that makes our visits to the groves so delightful by his gambols and chatterings. The squirrel, however, does his work of gathering corn and nuts during the day, and, like an honest man, sleeps at night contented and happy, while the rat is prowling about pantry and granary to plunder and destroy. The tail of the rat is a hand to reach into a jar of sweetmeats and draw out its contents, and a staff to steady himself by, while the tail of a squirrel curled over his back is an umbrella by day and a blanket at night.

2. Squirrels are at home in the forest. Their agility is extreme, and they never seem to rest. If seen for a moment in one place, like a flash of light they appear to flit to another. We see them passing incessantly from branch to branch, from tree to tree, or again they jump to the ground from so great a height as to threaten their destruction. But these leaps do not injure them, for they continue their play as if nothing had happened. The

broad, bushy tail acts as a wing, and, in some measure, supports them in the air, breaking the force of their fall.

3. The squirrel lives upon nuts, acorns, corn, and fruit. The pert little rascal has a habit, also, of robbing birds' nests, and sucking the eggs which he finds. Sometimes an old blackbird catches him in the midst of his feast, and gives him a drubbing which he remembers until his hide gets well. The squirrel builds a nice, warm, dry nest of moss and leaves, among the branches, or in some hollow tree or log, and he always keeps it clean. Near the nest he lays up his winter store of nuts; and upon pleasant days he awakens from his long nap, takes a bite, and goes to sleep again.

4. Squirrels live in pairs. The nest is made large enough for father, mother, and three or four young ones. Sometimes a pair build three or four nests at convenient distances from one another. Upon the appearance of danger the residence is changed. In the morning the mother squirrel takes the family out to exercise, but, if any intruder appears, she carries them off with great rapidity to one of her other homes. Squirrels are among the prettiest of household pets, and they may become so tame as to have entire liberty to go and come as they please, only it is difficult to keep them out of the jaws of the cat and the dog.

5. However, this is not always the case. A tiny squirrel was adopted by a lady in a Western mining-camp, who tells the following story: " The camp already contained, in the way of pets, three dogs, two cats, a fawn, and a hawk. By the side of any of these creatures the poor little *Ardea*, as my Mexican woman called him, was a mere pygmy. His great delight was to curl himself in a ball and take a comfortable nap in my hand. Should

his slumbers be disturbed by any undue movement, I was admonished by a nip of his sharp little teeth.

6. "All the members of the happy family were taught to respect his rights, save Peep, the hawk. The three dogs—Grouse, the setter; Roxy, the black-and-tan; and Prince, the bull-dog—eyed the new-comer suspiciously, and once or twice, at an opportune moment, made a spring toward him; but he retreated in a masterly way to an inaccessible corner, and the dogs were taught better manners by a sharp touch of my riding-whip.

7. "Very funny were the little creature's encounters with the kittens. He kept them at bay by turning on his back and fighting with tooth and claw when too hard pressed. Both learned to respect his rights, and at last the three became great friends. Frequently the squirrel was found curled up asleep between his two former enemies.

8. "The fawn, our most dainty pet, with his beautiful soft eyes, and his gentle ways, who also was called by his Spanish name, *Venado*, was adopted by Ardea, as his foster-mother, and he found great comfort in tucking himself away in the soft fur of the fawn, when Venado was placidly chewing his cud. The little autocrat did not hesitate to assert himself, if disturbed, by biting the fawn's nose, who soon learned to accept his fate with quiet endurance.

9. "Only Peep was incorrigible. He watched most eagerly from his perch outside the window, and almost twisted his head from his body when Ardea scampered about on the dining-table, daintily picking up crumbs, and sitting up in the quaintest fashion, with a piece of macaroni, or some other morsel, in his paws. When exasperated beyond bounds, Peep would take a desperate flight as far as his string permitted, and, failing to make a capture, return discomfited to his perch on the railing.

10. "One morning Ardea was missing, and, after a vain search about the house, a hunt in all his favorite nooks, we were almost in despair of finding him. Before giving up all hope we walked around the long piazza, and at the very end discovered Peep, in jubilant mood, his cord stretched taut, one claw thrust out, while just beyond his reach crouched naughty little trembling Ardea."

11. Another rodent common to our woods is the porcupine, which we have already described. In Africa and Asia the porcupine is about the same size as ours, but has much longer quills. It lives on herbs and fruit, and comes out at night to seek its food. When attacked, it rolls itself up in a ball and thrusts out its sharp quills, which are from eight to ten inches long. While in this position none but very hungry animals care to attack it. It is said that the puma has a curious way of disposing of the American porcupine. He seizes it by the head, and making a slit across the pate, where there are no quills, he gradually draws the carcass out of the skin.

12. The beaver, one of the larger rodents, is among the most interesting of animals. A full account of its appearance and habits is given in Book I. Beavers live in communities, build dams across streams to keep the water above at a uniform height, and in the pond thus formed they build houses, with upper chambers above the water, and dry for their nests. The entrance to the dwellings is always under the water. In building dams they gnaw off large trees, cut logs of proper length, and float them down to the place where the dam is to be constructed. When the skeleton of the dam is completed, it is finished by plastering the crevices with mud. The beaver is easily tamed, and becomes a kind, affectionate, and clean member of the household, and the only trouble is his propensity to make a dam across the corner of the

drawing-room with the coal-scuttle and chairs, and to provide other material for the purpose by gnawing off the legs of the table.

13. Among the larger rodents, the marmots are the

The Beaver.

most widely distributed and the best known. They are larger than the common rabbit, and have a heavy body and short legs, armed with sharp claws. They dig burrows deep in the earth, each of which has several entrances, so that in case of invasion they can escape. Their food consists of grass, clover, and tender herbage of various kinds. The European marmot has his home high up in the Alps, or in the cold regions of the North. They live in communities, and, when out feeding, they put sentinels to give warning of approaching danger. In November they fill their deep, dry burrows with hay, close the entrance, and, covering themselves snugly in bed, they go to sleep until the next April.

14. The American marmot is known generally as the woodchuck, but is called ground-hog in the South and West. It is somewhat larger than its European cousin, but has the same general appearance and habits. It does not live in so large communities, but usually two or more are found together, one of which watches while the others feed. In consequence of a warmer climate, its burrows are less deep than those of its Alpine kin, and its winter nap is not so long.

CUFF AND THE WOODCHUCK.

1. I knew a farmer in New York who had a very large bob-tailed churn-dog, by the name of Cuff. The farmer kept a large dairy, and made a great deal of butter; and it was the business of Cuff to spend nearly the half of each summer day treading the endless round of the churning-machine. During the remainder of the day he had plenty of time to sleep and rest, and sit on his hips, and survey the landscape.

2. One day, sitting thus, he discovered a woodchuck about forty rods from the house, on a steep hill-side, feeding about near his hole, which was beneath a large rock. The old dog, forgetting his stiffness, and remembering the fun he had had with the woodchucks in his earlier days, started off at his highest speed, vainly hoping to catch this one before he could get to his hole. But the woodchuck, seeing the dog come laboring up the hill, sprang to the mouth of his den, and, when his pursuer was only a few rods off, whistled tauntingly, and went in.

3. This occurred several times, the old dog marching up the hill, and then marching down again, having had his labor for his pains. I suspect that he revolved the subject in his mind, while he revolved the great wheel of the churning-machine, and that some turn or other

brought him a happy thought, for next time he showed himself a strategist. Instead of giving chase to the woodchuck, when first discovered, he crouched down to the ground, and, resting his head on his paws, watched him. The woodchuck kept working away from his hole, lured by the tender clover, but, not unmindful of his safety, lifted himself up on his haunches every few moments, and surveyed the approaches.

4. Presently, after the woodchuck had let himself down from one of these attitudes of observation, and resumed his feeding, Cuff started swiftly but stealthily up the hill, precisely in the attitude of a cat when she is stalking a bird. When the woodchuck rose up again, Cuff was perfectly motionless, and half hid by the grass. When he again resumed his clover, Cuff sped up the hill as before, this time crossing a fence, but in a low place, and so nimbly that he was not discovered. Again the woodchuck was on the lookout, again Cuff was motionless and hugging the ground. As the dog nears his victim he is partially hidden by a swell in the earth, but still the woodchuck, from his outlook, reports "All right!" when Cuff, having not twice as far to run as the 'chuck, throws all stealthiness aside, and rushes directly for the hole. At that moment the woodchuck discovers his danger, and, seeing that it is a race for life, leaps as I never saw marmot leap before. But he is two seconds too late; his retreat is cut off, and the powerful jaws of the old dog close upon him.

5. The next season Cuff tried the same tactics again with like success; but, when the third woodchuck had taken up his abode at the fatal hole, the old churner's wits and strength had begun to fail him, and he was baffled in each attempt to capture the animal.

CHAPTER XIV.

LONG EARS AND THEIR KIN.

1. ANOTHER group of the rodents includes the rabbits and the hares. Their jaws and teeth are shaped for gnawing, like the squirrel's, but their food consists mainly of tender plants and the bark of trees. The only harm they do is when they get into the vegetable-garden and feast upon the cabbage and lettuce, or when, in winter, they are driven by hunger to gnaw the bark from young fruit-trees.

2. Rabbits live in communities, and have their homes in burrows which they dig in the ground. The nests are separate, but the burrows open into one another, and a rabbit village, or "warren," often contains hundreds of passages, with great numbers of doors opening into the outer air. A rabbit entering any one of these doors easily finds his way to his own nest.

3. Both rabbits and hares are timid animals, and they have no means of defense against their enemies. Their only safety is in flight. To enable them to detect the presence of a foe, they are furnished with large, sensitive ears, and they can hear the least cracking of a twig or the faintest rustle of a blade of dry grass. The silent creeping of a weasel, the stealthy tread of a cat, or the noiseless flight of the owl fail to make an impression which the large ears can gather in, and this harmless clover-nibbler falls a prey to these savage foes.

4. Rabbits increase with great rapidity. It is estimated that, if unmolested, a single pair of rabbits in four years would produce 1,250,000. If not kept down by cats, dogs, weasels, owls, hawks, and foxes, they would soon overrun a country. Rabbits were introduced into New Zealand,

where their natural enemies did not exist. They multiplied so fast that they threatened to devour the entire crops of the country. They were caught in traps by the thousand, but their numbers did not sensibly diminish, until multitudes of dogs, cats, and ferrets, wild and tame, were let loose upon them.

5. The hare does not live in communities like the rabbit, but leads a solitary life. His home is in the open fields, away from bush, copse, or hedge, which may be used as a possible hiding-place for a foe. Here he sits, with his legs folded under him, and the grass gradually accommodates itself to the shape of his body, making his "form." In winter the snow covers him and keeps him from freezing. Here, away as far as possible from his enemies, he stays, venturing out only to get food, and keeping his large ears wide open for the least shadow of a sound.

6. In America we have none of the true burrowing rabbits. All American rabbits are really hares, living solitary lives and having homes in grassy "forms," or in crevices among rocks and logs. The common rabbit is small, gray, timid, and wild. It is never tamed and made into a household pet like its European cousin. It multiplies rapidly, but it is caught and eaten by its enemies with equal rapidity; so it just about holds its own.

7. Dr. Coues says: "The prairies of the West furnish several species of hares of great size, with very long legs and extravagant ears. All of these are indiscriminately known, in the vernacular of the regions they respectively inhabit, as 'jack-rabbits,' or 'jackass-rabbits,' in contradistinction from the several kinds of smaller, shorter-eared and shorter-legged species commonly called 'cotton-tails,' or 'sage-rabbits.' The Northern species is distinguished, among other things, by having the top of the tail white, or nearly so, like its under sur-

face. It also turns nearly pure white in winter, as the other jack-rabbits do not.

8. "In noting the habitat of the prairie hare, we must

The Jack-Rabbit.

exclude all wooded regions from the range. Emphatically a creature of the plains, it probably never enters timber, though it may range up to the very edge of the woods, and even be found in the brush along the river-bottoms. This hare is not gregarious, but roams in solitude over the broad, rolling prairie, where the antelope and the buffalo range. As we measure the weary miles of a day's march, suddenly the great jack springs from under our feet and goes bounding off with those wonderful leaps.

9. "The female does not burrow, as most prairie mammals are wont to do, but constructs a simple "form" in the grass, beneath some thick, low bush or tuft of weeds. The young are agile little creatures, even when only a week or two old, and hard to catch. This hare is little esteemed by most persons, either for its flesh or its fur, and is seldom pursued; in a country where buffalo, elk, deer, and antelope abound, the pursuit of a 'jack-rabbit' is considered ridiculous. The Indians, however, eat it, as they do everything else that they can chew and swallow, and it is sometimes netted by them in great numbers, after a peculiar fashion, when these people turn out by hundreds for the battue.

10. "The extraordinary agility of this animal, which would be inferred from inspection of its lithe yet muscular and free-limbed shape, has always excited attention. The early travelers, Lewis and Clarke, speak of its leaping some eighteen or twenty feet at one bound, and think this probably no exaggeration. To one who has never seen the creatures alive it is difficult to give an idea of the extraordinary spectacle they offer when running at full speed, and the way they get over the ground is wonderful, considering how much force is expended in the height of the leap.

11. "The first sign one usually has of a jack, which has squatted in hopes of being passed unnoticed till its fears forced it to fly, is a great bound into the air, with straightened-out body and erected ears. The instant the animal touches the ground again it is up in the air for the second time, with a peculiar springy jerk, more like the bouncing of a ball, apparently, than the result of muscular motion. It scarcely seems to fairly touch the ground

to gather itself for the next leap, but holds its legs stiffly extended, as if to rebound by force of the concussion.

12. "With a succession of these great jerky leaps the animal makes straight away, having nothing of the dodging about and the scuttling around bushes that marks the course of the little sage-rabbit. I have occasionally had both these kinds of hares running before me at once, and nothing could be more different than their appearance. As the jack gains on a pursuer, or as its fears subside, the springs grow shorter, lower, and weaker, just as a flat stone skipped along the surface of water shortens and lowers in rebounding, till finally the animal squats on its haunches with a last jerk, and comes to a stock-still to look or listen. If entirely reassured, it may then lope on with easy steps till out of sight, or it may squat and disappear—to which latter end it is only necessary to pin the ears back, when the animal goes out of sight.

13. "If there is anything more curious about a jack than its legs and the way it runs, it is the ears and the way it hides. If a jack would only keep still and never hoist its ears, it would conduce to longevity; for these enormous appendages are, curiously, the most conspicuous parts of the whole animal; and the natural timidity and watchfulness of the jack are so great that the ears almost always stand on the alert. When squatting closely, with ears folded back flat, the animal may be almost stepped on without being noticed, so closely do its colors blend with the surroundings.

14. "The attitude it assumes when on the watch is highly characteristic. It is drawn up to its full height, sitting on its haunches, with one fore-foot advanced before the other, and the ears parted in opposite directions; under these circumstances the slightest stimulation of its fears is enough to send it bounding off."

15. Mark Twain describes this animal as follows: "As the sun was going down, we saw the first specimen of an animal known, from Kansas clear to the Pacific Ocean, as the 'jackass-rabbit.' He is well named. He is just like any other rabbit, except that he is from one third to twice as large, has longer legs in proportion to his size, and has the most preposterous ears that ever were mounted on any creature but a jackass.

16. "When he is sitting quiet, thinking about his sins, or is absent-minded or unapprehensive of danger, his majestic ears project above him conspicuously; but the breaking of a twig will scare him nearly to death, and then he tilts back his ears gently and starts for home. All you can see, then, for the next minute, is his long, gray form stretched out straight, and 'streaking it' through the low sage-brush, head erect, eyes right, and ears just canted a little to the rear, but showing you where the animal is all the time, the same as if he carried a jib.

17. "Now and then he makes a marvelous spring with his long legs, high over the stunted sage-brush, and scores a leap that would make a horse envious. Presently he comes down to a long, graceful lope, and shortly he disappears. He has crouched behind a sage-bush, and will sit there and listen and tremble, until you get within six feet of him, when he will get under way again.

18. "But one must shoot at this creature once, if he wishes to see him throw his heart into his heels, and do the best he knows how. He is frightened clear through, and he lays his long ears down on his back, straightens himself out like a yard-stick every spring he makes, and scatters miles behind him with an easy indifference that is enchanting.

19. "Our whole party shot at this specimen and made

him 'hump' himself. It is not putting it too strong to say that he was frantic. He dropped his ears, set up his tail, and left for San Francisco at a speed which can only be described as a flash and a vanish. Long after he was out of sight we could hear him whiz."

CHAPTER XV.

BIRD-LANGUAGE.

1. ONE day, in the bluest of summer weather,
    Sketching under a whispering oak,
   I heard five bobolinks laughing together
    Over some ornithological joke.

2. What the fun was I couldn't discover;
    Language of birds is a riddle on earth;
   What could they find in white-weed and clover
    To split their sides with such musical mirth?

3. Was it some prank of the prodigal summer,
    Face in the cloud or voice in the breeze,
   Querulous cat-bird, woodpecker drummer,
    Cawing of crows high over the trees?

4. Was it some chipmunk's chatter, or weasel
    Under the stone-wall stealthy and sly?
   Or was the joke about me at my easel,
    Trying to catch the tints of the sky?

5. Still they flew tipsily, shaking all over,
    Bubbling with jollity, brimful of glee,
   While I sat listening, deep in the clover,
    Wondering what their jargon could be.

6. 'Twas but the voice of a morning the brightest
    That ever dawned over yon shadowy hills;
   'Twas but the song of all joy that is lightest—
    Sunshine breaking in laughter and trills.

7. Vain to conjecture the words they are singing;
    Only by tones can we follow the tune
   In the full heart of the summer fields ringing,
    Ringing the rhythmical gladness of June!

C. P. Cranch.

CHAPTER XVI.

THE MONARCH OF THE MOUNTAIN.

1. While in the wilds the lion is lord of the plains, the tiger is sovereign in the jungles, and the jaguar has sway in Amazonian forests, the bear is the undisputed monarch of the mountains and of the cold regions of the North. Wolves hunt in packs and become the terror of frontier settlements, and yet in size, strength, and courage, the wolf is greatly inferior to the bear. The bear is found in every part of the world except in Australia, and even there an animal is found, half monkey, half bear. The several species of bears, while differing in size and strength, are much alike in general appearance and habits.

2. The bear usually has a rough, shaggy coat, massive hind-quarters, a peculiar gait, and a habit of standing erect upon his hind-feet when fighting with an enemy. The clumsy gait is a consequence of his plantigrade structure. The long lower joint of the hind-leg strikes flat upon the ground, and the animal seems to shuffle along rather than to walk. The feet are armed with long, sharp, protruding

Snug Quarters.

claws, and these, impelled by powerful muscles, are capable of inflicting terrible wounds.

3. The bear is both carnivorous and graminivorous, thriving equally well on animal or vegetable diet. Most of the species are good climbers and swimmers. It is sociable with its own kind, and shows a strong attachment to its mate and young. Except in a few species, it is harmless when undisturbed; but it becomes ferocious and dangerous when attacked or when defending its family. It wards off blows with great dexterity, and returns them with interest. In a fight it rears itself upon its hind-feet, gives the "bear-hug," and uses the claws of its hind-feet with terrible effect. When taken young it is easily tamed, and for a year or more it is as playful and harmless as a young puppy; but later it must be restrained, for fear of accidents.

4. In the cold regions, bears sleep or hibernate in the winter. During the fall they become very fat, and, when the winter comes in earnest, they cease feeding, retire to their den in some secure and sheltered place in rocks or hollow trees, curl themselves up, and remain until spring in a condition resembling sleep, but with the vital forces more fully suspended than in real sleep. The stomach contracts, the blood moves slowly, and every function of the body goes on in a languid way. The little food necessary to support this feeble life is furnished by the fat. It was once believed that the bear is nourished during the winter by sucking his own claws. The warmth of spring arouses him from his lethargy, and he comes out of his den in full strength for his summer's work.

5. The American black bear has always been a favorite theme of story among both white and red men. It has been found in all the States from Maine to Florida. The climate of the Northern and Middle States seems to

be well adapted to the nature of the animal, although individuals differ somewhat in size and shape even in the same localities; some having shorter legs, shorter body, the head broad and flat between the ears, and a short peaked muzzle of light gray color, while others have longer legs, longer body, a head equally broad between the ears, but more rounded, longer, and larger, and the muzzle of brown color. It is a formidable antagonist when wounded or provoked, but seldom makes battle when allowed to escape. It has wonderful vitality, and, to use a hunter's phrase, will carry off more lead than any other animal.

6. "I believe that an old lean bear can travel more miles over a rough country in the space of one week than any other wild animal. The gray wolf might gain a few lengths during the first three days, but at the end of the week I think the bear would come out several miles ahead. Who ever heard of a lean bear tiring down? Let him thoroughly understand that he has got to go, and he will lead off a race that will surprise both men and dogs. When closely pursued by dogs, he has a peculiar trick of changing ends; that is, making a sudden whirl rearward, and woe to the unlucky dog that is within the sweep of his murderous paw! This sudden turn causes a momentary halt among the pack, while the speed of the bear doesn't seem to be diminished, and he gets about a quarter of a mile the start before the dogs begin to comprehend the trick.

7. "The bear can subsist on very short allowance, and will thrive fast when food is plenty, and at such times will frequently become extremely fat, when he becomes a more easy prey to the hunters. The flesh of the bear, when fattened on mast, is of excellent quality and fine flavor, and was highly prized by the early frontier inhabitants.

He is not carnivorous by nature, but in the absence of vegetable diet will eat mutton and young pork with evident relish. He will tear the bark from rotten or decayed logs in search of snails, grubs, and worms, which he eats with avidity. He destroys wasps' and humble-bees' nests; will demolish ant-hills, simply for the small amount of sustenance contained in their eggs; but his natural food is esculent roots and nuts of all kinds, blackberries, whortleberries, black cherries, and wild fruits of all kinds; also green corn in the milk."

8. The brown bear is found all over Europe and Asia. It is somewhat larger than the black bear of America, but in character and disposition they are much alike. The natural diet of the brown bear consists of vegetable substances, honey, and the larvæ of ants; but, having once tasted pork, he generally hangs around the farm yard until he falls a victim to the wrath of the farmer. Like his American cousin, he is easily tamed, but becomes dangerous if given his liberty after he has attained his full growth. Both the black and the brown bear hibernate in the North, but not in the South. The following story, of a tame bear in Sweden, gives a very good idea of the character of this brown Bruin:

9. "The cub was captured in its den when about three weeks old. Being fed with warm milk, young Bruin throve satisfactorily, and, when large enough to enjoy liberty, he usually stayed in the yard with the bear-dog "Jeppe," playing and springing about his companion like a cat. He was also much attached to his master, delighting to accompany him not only to the forest, where he often clambered up trees, but also into the house, where removing chairs and tables from one room into another appeared to be his favorite occupation. Strangers always received his attentions; but as these were somewhat

brusque, and expressed in a surly tone, they tended rather to repel than attract.

10. "One day, while Bruin was yet of tender years, a kitten came into the yard and immediately drew his surprised attention upon herself; but young puss, not admiring his looks, first cast upon him an angry glance, and then sprang up and fixed her claws in his head, exciting such alarm that he trotted off in nervous haste, and hid himself in an outhouse. Afterward he always fled at the sight of this cat, though she was the only one of which he showed fear.

11. "Whenever he could intrude into the kitchen he bemeaned himself like an officious and meddlesome husband, disordering affairs, greatly to the vexation of the domestics, to whose castigations with a stout knob-stick he payed little regard. One day he laid hold of a coffee-pan that stood on the hearth, and was conveying it in his paws to the yard, when the hot contents, overflowing on his bosom, provoked him to cast it on the ground and flatten it with a stroke of his paw.

12. "As he grew older it was found necessary to impose some check upon his movements, and for this purpose a chain, with a log at the end of it, was attached to a collar round his neck. Such badge of servitude and interference with the liberty of a free-born bear was not to be borne. At first he tried to strike off the log with his paws; then he dragged it to the river, but was vastly irritated to find that, after every attempt to sink it, the audacious log came to the surface again. Finally he dug a hole, put the log into it, and replaced the earth, stamping or pressing it down; then, apparently satisfied with his work, he attempted to move off, but found himself in a worse fix than before; however, after sundry angry jerks the chain broke, and he regained his freedom, leaving his incumbrance in the grave.

13. "Poor Bruin! after his winter's nap he must indeed have got up on the wrong side of the bed, for he became so unbearably troublesome and subject to such angry moods, that, at the early age of about three years, he was doomed to death, and executed accordingly."

14. The largest and most savage of all bears is the grizzly, of the Rocky Mountains and Pacific coast. He is a flesh-eater, and does not hesitate to attack man or beast. He is hard to kill, and very dangerous when wounded. Bullets are fatal only when they pierce his heart or brain, and an instance is related of a bear that lived twenty minutes with two bullets through his heart. With his enormous size and long plantigrade foot, the gait of the grizzly has much more of the shuffle than other bears, and it seems that he trots with his fore-feet and drags his hind-quarters. But he goes over the ground with great speed, and a man on foot would stand a poor chance to get out of his way.

15. This is the story which an old hunter tells of a grizzly: "One day I rode out alone, armed with my rifle. In the midst of a plain, covered with wild clover, I saw a grizzly rolling on the soft herbage, with his paws playing stupidly in the air. The cattle not far distant were watching this movement, and a bull advanced toward it, drawn, it seemed to me, by curiosity. The bull gradually drew nearer the bear, the herd following him, grazing as they went. He forced his way through the tall clover until he came within fifty yards, bellowing and tearing up the earth. The bear moved less, only now and then rolling a little to stir the field.

16. "The curiosity of the bull now changed into anger; he came slowly up, snorting and bellowing, and at length stepped suddenly forward and plunged at the bear, who caught him in his powerful arms and held him

THE MONARCH OF THE MOUNTAIN. 99

down. There was fifteen minutes' struggling and roaring, and the two immense beasts rolled over and over, crushing flat a wide area in the field. The herd gathered around, and bellowed with rage and terror; but the bear never slackened his hold until the bull was exhausted and ceased to strive. Then up rose Bruin as light as a cat, and the herd ran bellowing to the hills. While the bear was feasting on his prey, I rode up and put a bullet through his heart."

17. The polar bear is a rival of the grizzly in size, strength, and ferocity. Its usual weight is from eight

The Polar Bear.

hundred to one thousand pounds, but an occasional one has been killed weighing twelve hundred to fifteen hundred pounds. Its color is a silvery white, with a slight yellowish hue, varying with different individuals. Its home is among the snow and ice of the extreme North, and it is necessarily carnivorous, as no vegetation grows in the regions it inhabits. It lives on fish and seals, and it discovers a great deal of sagacity in capturing its prey. Observing a seal basking on the rocks near the shore, it dives into the water and swims out so as to cut off the retreat of the seal and obliges him to take to the land. Here escape is impossible, and the bear indulges in an unctuous feast, which it shares with the other members of its family. The following narrative, showing the affection of the white bear for its young, is from the "Journal of a Voyage for making Discoveries to the North Pole":

18. "Early in the morning, the man at the mast-head gave notice that three bears were making their way very fast over the ice, and that they were directing their course toward the ship. They had, without question, been invited by the scent of the blubber of a sea-horse—killed a few days before—which the men had set on fire, and which was burning on the ice at the time of their approach.

19. "They proved to be a she-bear and her two cubs; but the cubs were nearly as large as the dam. They ran eagerly to the fire, and drew out from the flames part of the flesh of the sea-horse that remained unconsumed, and ate it voraciously. The crew from the ship threw great lumps of the flesh of the sea-horse, which they had still left, upon the ice. These the old bear carried away singly, laid every lump before her cubs as she brought it, and, dividing it, gave each a share, reserving but a small portion to herself.

20. "As she was taking away the last piece, the men leveled their muskets at the cubs, and shot them both

dead; and, in her retreat, they wounded the dam, but not mortally. It would have drawn tears of pity from any but unfeeling minds to mark the affectionate concern expressed by this poor beast, in the last moments of her expiring young. Though she was sorely wounded, and could but just crawl to the place where they lay, she carried the lump of flesh which she had fetched away and placed it before them. Seeing that they refused to eat, she laid her paws first upon one and then upon the other, and endeavored to raise them up. It was pitiful to hear her moan.

21. "When she found she could not stir them, she went off, and, stopping when she had got to some distance, she looked back and moaned. When she found that she could not entice them away, she returned, and, smelling around them, began to lick their wounds. She went off a second time as before, and, having crawled a few paces, looked again behind her, and for some time stood moaning. But still her cubs not rising to follow her, she returned to them again, and, with signs of inexpressible fondness, went round one and round the other, pawing them and moaning. Finding at last that they were cold and lifeless, she raised her head toward the ship and growled at the murderers, who then shot her with a volley of musket-balls. She fell between her cubs, and died licking their wounds."

CHAPTER XVII.

HOW I KILLED A BEAR

1. So many conflicting accounts have appeared about my casual encounter with an Adirondack bear, last summer, that, in justice to the public, to myself, and to the bear, it is necessary to make a plain statement of the facts. Besides, it is so seldom I have occasion to kill a bear, that the celebration of the exploit may be excused.

2. The encounter was accidental on both sides. I was

The Black Bear.

not hunting for a bear, and I have no reason to suppose that a bear was looking for me. The fact is, that we were both out blackberrying, and met by chance—the usual way. There is among the Adirondack visitors always a great deal of conversation about bears—a general expression of the wish to see one in the woods, and much speculation as to how a person would act, if he or she chanced to meet one. But bears are scarce and timid, and appear only to a favored few.

3. It was a warm day in August, just the sort of day when an adventure of any kind seemed impossible. But it occurred to the housekeepers of our cottage to send me to the clearing, on the mountain back of the house, to pick blackberries. It was rather a series of small clearings, running up into the forest, much overgrown with bushes and briers, and not unromantic. Cows pastured there, penetrated through the leafy passages from one opening to another, and browsing among the bushes. I was kindly furnished with a six-quart pail, and told not to be gone long.

4. Not from any predatory instinct, but, to save appearances, I took a gun. It adds to the manly aspects of a person with a tin pail, if he also carries a gun. It was possible I might start up a partridge; though how I was to hit him, if he started up instead of standing still, puzzled me. I prefer the rifle: it makes a clean job of death. The rifle was Sharp's—an excellent weapon, belonging to a friend of mine, who had intended, for a good many years back, to kill a deer with it. He could hit a tree with it—if the wind did not blow, and the atmosphere was just right, and the tree was not too far off—nearly every time. Of course, the tree must have some size.

5. In this blackberry-patch, bears had been seen. The summer before, our colored cook, accompanied by a little girl, was picking berries there one day, when a bear came out of the woods, and walked toward them. The girl took to her heels and escaped. Aunt Chloe was paralyzed with terror. Instead of attempting to run, she sat down on the ground, and began to weep and to scream, giving

herself up as lost. The bear was bewildered by this conduct. He approached and looked at her; he walked around and surveyed her. Probably he had never seen a colored person before, and did not know whether she would agree with him. At any rate, after watching her a few moments, he turned about, and went into the forest.

6. When I had climbed the hill, I set my rifle against a tree, and began picking berries, lured on from bush to bush by the black gleam of the fruit, penetrating farther and farther through leaf-shaded cow-paths flecked with sunlight, into clearing after clearing. I could hear on all sides the tinkle of bells, the cracking of sticks, and the stamping of cattle that were taking refuge in the thicket from flies. Occasionally, as I broke through a covert, I encountered a meek cow, who stared at me stupidly for a second, and then shambled off into the brush. I became accustomed to this dumb society, and picked on in silence, attributing all the wood-noises to the cattle, thinking nothing of any real bear.

7. In point of fact, I was thinking of a nice, romantic bear, which I was weaving into a tale, the moral of which was to be kindness to animals, when I happened to look some rods away, to the outer edge of the clearing, and there was the bear. He was standing on his hind-legs, and doing just what I was doing—picking blackberries. With one paw he bent down the bush, while, with the other, he clawed the berries into his mouth—green ones and all. To say that I was astonished is inside the mark. I suddenly discovered that I didn't want to see a bear, after all.

8. At about the same moment the bear saw me, stopped eating berries, and regarded me with a glad surprise. It is all very well to imagine what you would

do under the circumstances. Probably you wouldn't do it: I didn't. The bear dropped down on his fore-feet, and came slowly toward me. Climbing a tree was no use with so good a climber in the rear. If I started to run, I had no doubt the bear would give chase; and, although a bear can not run down-hill as fast as he can run up-hill, yet I felt that he could get over this rough, brush-tangled ground faster than I could.

9. The bear was approaching. It suddenly occurred to me how I could divert his mind until I could fall back upon my military base. My pail was nearly full of excellent berries—much better than the bear could pick himself. I put the pail on the ground and slowly backed away from it, keeping my eye, as beast-tamers do, on the bear. The *ruse* succeeded.

10. The bear came up to the berries and stopped. Not accustomed to eat out of a pail, he tipped it over, and nosed about the fruit "gorming" it down, mixed with leaves and dirt, like a pig. The bear is a worse feeder than a pig. Whenever he disturbs a maple-sugar camp in the spring, he always upsets the buckets of sirup, and tramples round in the sticky sweets, wasting more than he eats. The bear's manners are thoroughly disagreeable.

11. As soon as my enemy's head was down, I started and ran. Somewhat out of breath, and shaky, I reached my faithful rifle. It was not a moment too soon. I heard the bear crashing through the brush after me. Enraged at my duplicity, he was now coming on with blood in his eye. I felt the time of one of us was probably short. The rapidity of thought at such moments of peril is well known. As I was cocking my gun, I made a hasty and unsatisfactory review of my whole life. I noted that, even in such a compulsory review, it is almost impossible

to think of any good thing you have done. The sins come out uncommonly strong. I recollected a newspaper subscription I had delayed paying, years and years ago, until both editor and newspaper were dead, and which now never could be paid to all eternity.

12. The bear was coming on. I tried to remember what I had read about encounters with bears. I couldn't recall an instance in which a man had run away from a bear in the woods and escaped, although I recalled plenty where the bear had run away from the man and got off. I tried to think what is the best way to kill a bear with a gun, when you are not near enough to club him with the stock. My first thought was to fire at his head, to plant the ball between his eyes: but this is a dangerous experiment. The bear's brain is very small, and, unless you hit that, the bear does not mind a bullet in his head—that is, not at the time. I remembered that the instant death of the bear would follow a bullet planted just back of his fore-leg, and sent into his heart. This spot is also difficult to reach, unless the bear stands offside toward you, like a target. I finally determined to fire at him generally.

13. The bear was coming on; he had, in fact, come on. I judged that he could see the white of my eyes. All my subsequent reflections are confused. I raised the gun, covered the bear's breast, and let drive. Then I turned and ran like a deer. I did not hear the bear pursuing. I looked back. The bear had stopped. He was lying down. I then remembered that the best thing to do after having fired your gun is to load it. I slipped in a charge, keeping my eye on the bear. He never stirred. I walked back suspiciously. There was a quiver in his hind-legs, but no other motion. Still he might be shamming: bears often sham. To make sure, I approached

and put a ball into his head. He didn't mind it now; he minded nothing. He was calm in death. In order that he might remain so, I blew his brains out, and then started for home. I had killed a bear!

14. I sauntered into the house with an unconcerned air. There was a chorus of voices: "Where are your blackberries?" "Why were you gone so long?" "Where is your pail?" "I left the pail!" "Left the pail? what for?" "A bear wanted it." "Oh, nonsense!" "Well, the last I saw of it, a bear had it." "Oh, come! You didn't really see a bear?" "Yes, but I really did see a real bear." "Did he run?" "Yes, he ran after me." "I don't believe a word of it! What did you do?" "Oh, nothing particular—except kill the bear." Cries of "Gammon!" "Don't believe it!" "Where is the bear?" "If you want to see the bear, you must go up into the woods. I couldn't bring him down alone."

15. Having satisfied the household that something extraordinary had occurred, I went down into the valley to get help. The great bear-hunter, who keeps one of the summer boarding-houses, received my story with a smile of incredulity; and the incredulity spread to the other inhabitants, and to the boarders, as soon as the story was known. However, as I insisted in all soberness, and offered to lead them to the bear, a party of forty or fifty people at last started off with me to bring the bear in. Nobody believed there was any bear in the case; but everybody who could get a gun carried one, and we went into the woods armed with guns, pistols, pitchforks, and sticks, against all contingencies and surprises—a crowd made up mostly of scoffers and jeerers.

16. But when I led the way to the fatal spot, and pointed out the bear, lying peacefully wrapped up in his own skin, something like terror seized the boarders, and

genuine excitement the natives. It was a no-mistake bear, by George! And the hero of the fight—well, I will not insist upon that. But what a procession that was carrying the bear home! and what a congregation was speedily gathered in the valley to see the bear! Our best preacher up there never drew anything like it on Sunday.

17. And I must say that my friends who were sportsmen behaved very well, on the whole. They didn't deny that it was a bear, although they said it was small for a bear. Mr. Drane, who is equally good with a rifle or rod, admitted that it was a very fair shot. But he needlessly remarked, after he had examined the wound in the bear, that he had seen that kind of shot made by a cow's horn. This kind of talk affected me not. When I went to sleep that night, my last delicious thought was, "I've killed a bear!"

Charles Dudley Warner.

CHAPTER XVIII.

THE BEAR IN FABLE AND STORY.

1. THE bear is so well known that he forms an important character in myth and fable, and enters largely into the common stories or folk-lore of the people in most countries and ages. In the mythology of the Norsemen he is made strong, majestic, and terrible, the god of thunder, the bear-king of storms. The tempest-demons, black-bearded, are his children, and the thunder-clouds go rolling and soaring and foaming overhead, bears every one of them, and close on the heels of their prey. In the East the bear is the shining one, the luminous sky. The Russian child hears, at the fireside, stories of the bear, in which he is shaggy and terrible, every hair of which is

Beech-nutting.

of iron; and again he is "the old man in the fur cloak." In Lapland the bear is the "dog of God," and among the peasants of the South he is mild and friendly, "the honey-finder." Science finds the "Great Bear" the most majestic object of the northern heavens, making its nightly march around the pole.

2. The good qualities of the bear, and the amiable side of his character, are represented in the stories which have become classic in children's literature. In "Beauty and the Beast," the terrible-appearing monster who took such excellent care of Beauty, and was so generous to her family, was a bear. Then there is the delightful story of "Snow-White and Rose-Red." The bear, hungry and cold, knocked at the door of the cottage on a wintry night, and was admitted by the kindly little girls. He was treated to a supper and a warm bed by the fireside, and became a welcome guest until spring. Afterward, when his two little friends were in distress and persecuted by an ill-tempered and malicious dwarf, the bear made his appearance at just the right moment, and with one blow of his paw put an end to the spiteful little manikin and his persecutions.

3. From very ancient times tame bears have been led over the country, until their awkward appearance and gait have become familiar. This has led to the idea that the bear is stupid as well as clumsy, and in story he is often made the victim of more crafty animals, especially the fox. This is well illustrated in the following:

WHY THE BEAR HAS A STUMPY TAIL.

4. One day the bear met the fox, who came creeping along with a string of fish he had stolen. "Whence did you get those from?" asked the bear. "O my Lord Bruin, I've been out fishing and caught them," said the

fox. So the bear had a mind to fish too, and bade the fox tell him how he was to set about it.

5. "Oh! it's an easy craft for you," answered the fox, "and soon learned. You've only to go upon the ice, and cut a hole and stick your tail down into it; and you must hold it there as long as you can. You mustn't mind if your tail smarts a little; that's when the fish bite. The longer you hold it there the more fish you will get; and then all at once out with it, with a cross-pull and with a strong pull too."

6. Yes: the bear did as the fox had said, and held his tail a long, long time down in the hole, till it was fast frozen in. Then he pulled it out with a cross-pull, and it snapped short off. That's why Bruin goes about with a stumpy tail this very day.

7. But the bear does not deserve this reputation for stupidity. "When it sets itself going after any one it wishes to catch, it displays an agility and address which those who have been hunted by it declare to be amazing. And when it wishes to get beetle-grubs out of the ground, ants out of their nest, honey out of a bee-tree, fruit from a slender bough, or birds' eggs out of a nest, it shows itself to be as ingenious and skillful as any other animal that has to live by its wits. To get, for instance, at the beetle-grubs, it scratches off the upper earth and then sucks them up out of the ground—an application of a scientific process which no animal without a prodigious reserve of air-force could hope to accomplish.

8. "When it wishes to empty an ant-hive it knocks the top off with its paws, and then, applying its mouth to the central gallery of the nest, inhales its breath forcibly, thereby setting up such a current of air that all the ants and their eggs come whirling up into his mouth like packets through a pneumatic tube. When robbing bees it

does not get stung, and when after wild apricots or acorns it not only balances itself with all the judgment of a rope-walker, but uses its weight very cleverly so as to bring other boughs within reach of its curved claws; nor while doing this does it conceal what it is about. On the contrary, when sucking at an ant-heap or grub-hole it makes such a noise that on a still evening it can be heard a quarter of a mile off, and when up a tree, and not alarmed, it goes smashing about among the boughs as if bears were not only the rightful lords of the manor, but as if there were no such things as enemies in the world."

9. The poet Merrick, in his desire to "point a moral and adorn a tale," rather overstates the effect of the sting of the bee upon the bear. The fact that it is always ready to plunder a new swarm, shows that it was not greatly injured by the old one. But here is the poem:

THE BEARS AND THE BEES.

10. "As two young bears in wanton mood,
Forth issuing from a neighboring wood,
Came where the industrious bees had stored
In artful cells their luscious hoard;
O'erjoyed they seized with eager haste,
Luxurious on the rich repast.
Alarmed at this the little crew
About their ears vindictive flew.
The beasts, unable to sustain
The unequal combat, quit the plain:
Half blind with rage and mad with pain,
Their native shelter they regain;
There sit, and, more discreeter grown,
Too late their rashness they bemoan.
And this by dear experience gain,
That pleasure's ever bought with pain.

So when the gilded parts of vice
Are placed before our longing eyes,
With greedy haste we snatch our fill
And swallow down the latent ill;
And when experience opes our eyes,
Away the fancied pleasure flies;
It flies, but oh! too late we find,
It leaves a real sting behind."

11. Æsop, in the fable, derives a lesson in morals and manners from another peculiarity of the bear. This is the fable:

THE BEAR AND THE TWO FRIENDS.

12. "Two friends, setting out together upon a journey which led through a dangerous forest, mutually promised to assist each other if they should happen to be assaulted. They had not proceeded far before they perceived a bear making toward them with great rage.

13. "There were no hopes in flight; but one of them, being very active, sprang up into a tree, upon which the other, throwing himself flat on the ground, held his breath and pretended to be dead, remembering to have heard it asserted that this creature will not prey upon a dead carcass. The bear came up, and, after smelling of him some time, left him and went on. When he was fairly out of sight and hearing, the hero from the tree called out, 'Well, my friend, what said the bear? He seemed to whisper you very closely.' 'He did so,' replied the other, 'and gave me this good advice, never to associate with a wretch who in the hour of danger will desert his friend.'"

14. The bear-stories of later date have little of the fancy which gave such a charm to those of the old time. Sometimes, however, they illustrate a point and have a quaint humor of their own. Here is the story of

THE BEAR AND THE POLITICIAN.

15. "I never but once," said Colonel Crockett, "was in what I call a genuine quandary. It was during my electioneering for Congress, at which time I strolled about in the woods so pestered by politics that I forgot my rifle. Any man may forget his rifle, you know, but it isn't every man who can make amends for it. It chanced that, as I was strolling along, the first thing that took my fancy was the snarling of some bears, which proceeded from the hollow of a tree; but I soon found that I could not reach the cubs with my hands, so I went feet foremost to see if I could draw them up by my toes. I hung on the top of the hole, straining with all my might to reach them, until at last my hands slipped, and down I went more than twenty feet to the bottom of that hole, and there I found myself almost knee-deep in a family of young bears.

16. "I soon found that I might as well undertake to climb up the steepest part of a rainbow as to get back—the hole in the tree being so large, and its sides so smooth and slippery. Now, this was a real, genuine, regular quandary. If I was to shout, it would have been doubtful whether they would hear me at the settlement, and if they did hear me the story would ruin my election; for a man that ventured into a place that he couldn't get himself out of, would forfeit the respect of the settlers. Well, now, while I was calculating whether it was best to shout for help or wait in the hole until after election, I heard a kind of grumbling and growling overhead, and looking I saw the old bear coming down stern foremost. As soon as she lowered herself within my reach I got a tight grip of her tail on my left hand, and with my little buck-hafted penknife in the other I commenced spurring her forward. No member of Congress rose quicker in the world than I

did! She took me out so quickly that it took my breath away, and the last I saw of her she was making a bee-line to the thickest part of the woods."

17. The next story, from California, exalts a new hero, and makes a victim of the bear. It has something of a wild Western flavor, and possibly will not bear the closest scrutiny:

THE BEAR AND THE BURRO.

18. "On Bull Creek, in Mariposa County, resides a Mr. Black, who is the possessor of a herd of cattle, which he regards as the apple of his eye. In the morning, before going to work, he would look fondly at them, as they walked out from the *corral* to go down to water; and, at evening, after supper, he would sit and smoke his pipe, and contemplate them, finding each day a new beauty in some favorite heifer, steer, or calf. They were fine cattle, and their owner was justly proud of them. None were sick; none died. They increased, flourished, and grew fat. In the winter, they fed upon the yellow grass upon the hill-side; in spring, when the gentle rains had caused the alfalfa to send up tender shoots, they stood knee-deep among the luxuriant and sweet-smelling herbage.

19. "But all this was too pleasant to last. A serpent entered Eden — and a grizzly bear Mr. Black's corral. Night after night the fattest and sleekest of the calves were ruthlessly torn from the sides of their helpless dams, and hurried away into the fastnesses of the mountains. Day after day their owner saw in the once mild and placid eyes of his herd a startled, hunted look—an expression of appeal which wrung his heart. Mr. Black was in despair, and, determined, at any cost, to be rid of this fiend of a bear, he published an advertisement offering a reward of fifty dollars to any person who would kill it.

20. "On Bull Creek, in Mariposa County, resides a

Mr. Opie, who is the possessor of a donkey, or *burro*, which is, no doubt, as dear to his owner as Mr. Black's horned cattle were to him. This burro, like most others, is fond of having his own way, and, when confined in stable or corral, and the idea occurs to him that he would prefer to extend his wanderings beyond those limits, he proceeds calmly to kick down the walls of the inclosure, and thoughtfully strolls away in search of drier sage-brush or more thorny greasewood. Now, it happened one night that Mr. Opie's burro, having, as usual, demolished the barriers between himself and freedom, strayed, in a meditative frame of mind, to the corral in which Mr. Black's cattle were confined. On reaching it, he gazed mildly at its occupants, and then gave himself up to a contemplation of the beauty of the scene.

21. "The clear stars looked down unwinkingly on the plain; high in the heavens rode the glorious moon. In the distance rose the mountains, bare near their base, but higher up clothed with chaparral, and higher still with dark pines. Scarcely a sound disturbed the quiet of the night. The long-drawn howl of the coyote was silent, but in the creek the water murmured softly its little song. All this the burro observed and enjoyed; but, as the sweet smell of the stacks reached his nostrils, he remembered that life was not made for dreaming, and, walking up to the corral, he leaned against it, and, with scarcely an effort, threw down half a dozen lengths of fence. Then he entered, and began to eat Mr. Black's hay.

22. "While all this was going on, a grizzly of remarkable size and ferocity was pursuing his way down a cañon toward the corral. He did not stop to contemplate the calm loveliness of the night, but went hurriedly along, for he was hungry, and he remembered a particularly large and fat calf that he had twice unsuccessfully tried to

catch. This time he vowed he would secure it. The corral reached, he found the fence down, and entering, looked about him. There, beyond the stacks, in the moonlight, reposed most of the cattle; but nearer, and in the shadow, he saw what he supposed to be the coveted fat calf.

23. "Quietly he slipped up behind it, and rose on his hind-feet to seize it, when suddenly a pair of heels flew up from the ground. One of these hit Bruin directly under the chin, breaking his jaw and teeth, and causing him to see more stars than were at that moment visible in the heavens; the other broke his right fore-leg. The patient burro then laid back his ears, and proceeded to further maltreat the unfortunate and astonished bear; and with so much energy did he carry on the assault that, in a short time, the wretched beast was chewed and kicked into those ursine happy hunting-grounds, where, it is to be presumed, the donkey brays not, and his long ears are never seen. The bear being dead, the burro went back to the stacks, and, as he munched Mr. Black's hay, meditated on the mutability of affairs upon this mundane sphere, and especially on the uncertainty of life."

CHAPTER XIX.

OUR SERVANTS OF STABLE AND HARNESS.

1. IN speaking of the horse, we can not but observe the improvement of American horses of to-day over those of a third of a century ago. Besides the thoroughbred or race-horse, and the trotter of famous record, there are becoming familiar among us the large draught-horses from Normandy, the Clydesdale from Scotland, the

Cleveland bay from England, the diminutive pony from the Shetland Islands, and the wiry little mustang from

Group of Horses.

our Western pampas. The horse among us is receiving a kinder and more intelligent treatment, in return for which he is giving a more valuable recompense in faithful service. Classed usually with the pachyderms, or thick-skinned animals, the horse, singular as it may seem, walks on his toe-nails, and these tips of his feet are formed into hard, firm hoofs, well adapted to hold the strong iron shoe, and to renew the waste occasioned by continued wear.

2. The common donkey is derived from the immense plains of the interior of Asia, and is known in nearly all

countries for his patience, endurance, and his ability to bear burdens and serve man in the craggy and steep mountain-defiles where horses can not go. Both he and his near relative, the mule, tough, nimble-footed, and docile, are more and more taking the place of the clumsy ox, and the more sensitive horse.

3. The zebra, whose home is in Africa, possesses most of the peculiar characteristics of the horse, but his wild nature never sufficiently yields to taming influences to make him a faithful servant. His quick and long sight, enabling him to discover approaching danger at a great distance, renders his capture very difficult. His beauty of form and color makes him an attractive object in the show and the zoölogical garden.

4. "By his physical structure," says "Chambers's Miscellany," "the horse is fitted for dry, open plains that yield a short, sweet herbage. His hoof is not adapted to the swamp; and though he may occasionally be seen browsing on tender shoots, yet he could subsist neither in the jungle nor in the forest. His lips and teeth, however, are admirably formed for cropping the shortest grass, and thus he luxuriates where many other herbivorous animals would starve, provided he be supplied with water, of which he is at all times a liberal drinker. He can not crush his food like the hippopotamus, nor does he ruminate like the ox; but he grinds the herbage with a peculiar lateral motion of the jaw which looks not unlike the action of the millstone.

5. "There is doubt expressed as to the original locality of the horse. The wild breeds of America are looked upon as the descendants of Spanish breeds imported by the first conquerors of that continent; those of the Ukraine in Europe are said to be the progeny of Russian horses abandoned after the siege of Azof, in 1696; and those of

Tartary are regarded as coming from a more southern stock. Naturalists, therefore, look to the countries bordering on Egypt as in all likelihood the primitive place of residence of this noble animal; and there is no doubt that the Arabian breed, when perfectly pure, presents the finest specimen of a horse in symmetry and graceful outline.

6. "Regarding the horse as of Asiatic origin, we now find him associated with man in almost every region of the habitable globe. Like the dog, ox, sheep, and a few others of the brute creation, he seems capable of accommodating himself to very different conditions, and assumes a shaggy coat or sleek skin, a size little inferior to the elephant, or not larger than that of an English mastiff, just as circumstances of climate and food require. His spirited fidelity as the servant of man is pictured by Byron, in his description of the horse of Mazeppa:

'The Cossack prince rubbed down his horse,
And made for him a leafy bed,
And smoothed his fetlocks and his mane,
And slacked his girth, and stripped his rein,
And joyed to see how well he fed;
For until now he had the dread
His wearied courser might refuse
To browse beneath the midnight dews;
But he was hardy as his lord,
And little cared for bed and board;
But spirited and docile too;
Whate'er was to be done, would do.
Shaggy and swift and strong of limb,
All Tartar-like he carried him;
Obeyed his voice, and came to call,
And knew him in the midst of all;
Though thousands were around—and night,
Without a star, pursued her flight—
That steed from sunset until dawn
His chief would follow like a fawn.'

7. "The endurance of the horse is great, and equaled only, perhaps, by that of the camel. The elephant either breaks down under his own weight or becomes infuriated when goaded beyond his accustomed powers; the ox, though extremely patient, suffers in his feet or becomes faint through hunger; but the horse toils on unflinchingly, till not unfrequently he drops down through mere exhaustion. The mares of the Bedouin Arabs will often travel fifty miles without stopping; and they have been known to go a hundred and twenty miles in extreme cases, with hardly a rest, and with no food. In 1804 an Arab horse at Bangalore, in the presidency of Madras, ran four hundred miles in the course of four successive days, and without showing any symptoms of more than ordinary fatigue.

8. "The affection of the horse is sometimes displayed in joyous gambols and familiar caresses like those of the dog, though, like the man in the fable, who was embraced by an ass, one would willingly dispense with such boisterous manifestations. We are informed, in the 'Sporting Magazine,' that a gentleman in Buckinghamshire had in his possession, in December, 1793, a three-year-old colt, a dog, and three sheep, which were his constant attendants in all his walks. When the parlor-window, which looked into the field, was open, the colt had often been known to leap through it, go up to and caress his master, and then leap back to his pasture."

9. Lamartine, in his "Pilgrimage to the Holy Land," records a story that a son of a sheik related to him, which shows the tender affection existing between the Arabs and their horses: "An Arab and his tribe had attacked a caravan of Damascus in the desert. The victory was complete, and the Arabs were already occupying themselves in arranging their rich booty, when the cavalry of the

pasha, who were sent to meet the caravan, fell at once on the victorious ravagers, killed a vast number, and made prisoners of the rest, whom they bound with cords and led to Acre as a present to the pasha. Abou-el-Masch, the name of the Arab chief, had received a ball in his arm during the combat; as the wound was mortal, the Turks had fastened him upon a camel, and, having seized upon his horse, led both on the way. The evening of the day they were to have reached Acre, they encamped with their prisoners among the mountains.

10. " The wounded Arab had his legs fastened by a leather strap, and was stretched near the tent where the Turks were sleeping. During the night, being kept awake through the anguish of his wound, he heard the neighing of his horse among the other steeds fastened around the tents, according to the custom of the Orientals. He recognized his voice, and, unable to resist the desire of speaking once more to the companion of his life, he painfully dragged himself along the ground, and succeeded, on his hands and knees, in reaching his beloved courser.

11. " ' Poor valued friend,' said he, ' what will become of thee among the Turks? Thou wilt be imprisoned under the ceiling of a khan, with the horses of an aga or pasha; no more will the women and the children carry thee camel's milk, and grains of barley and of doura in the palms of their hands; no more wilt thou gallop freely in the desert like the wind of Egypt; no more will thy broad chest divide the waters of Jordan, or thy sleek skin be refreshed by them, white as thy foam; at least, though I am become a slave, be thou free as air; there, go! return to the tent thou knowest; go tell my wife that Abou-el-Masch will behold her no more; and pass thy head between the curtains of the tent to lick the hands of my little ones.'

12. "Thus saying, Abou-el-Masch gnawed with his teeth the cord of goats' hair with which the Arabs fetter their horses. The animal was free! But, seeing his wounded master in bonds at his feet, the intelligent and faithful courser, with that natural instinct which no language could have explained to him, bowed down his head and smelled of his master; then, seizing him by the leather belt around his waist, set off on the full gallop, and carried him even to his tents. Having reached them, and thrown his master on the sand at the feet of his wife and children, the noble horse expired with fatigue. All the tribe wept over him; the poets sang his praises; and his name is honored from tongue to tongue by the Arabs of Jericho."

CHAPTER XX.

KAWEAH'S RUN.

1. AFTER trying hard to climb Mount Whitney, without success, and having returned to the plains, I enjoyed my two days' rest in hot Visalia, where were fruits and people. Everybody was of interest to me, not excepting the two Mexican mountaineers, who monopolized the agent at Wells, Fargo & Co.'s office, causing me delay. They were transacting some little item of business, and stood loafing by the counter, mechanically jingling huge spurs and shrugging their shoulders as they chatted in a dull, sleepy way. At the door they paused, keeping up quite a lively dispute, without apparently noticing me as I drew a small bag of gold and put it in my pocket. There was no especial reason why I should remark the

stolid, brutal cast of countenances, as I thought them not worse than the average California greasers.

2. I observed them enough to see that the elder was a man of middle height, of wiry, light figure, and thin, harsh visage; a certain angular sharpness making itself noticeable about the shoulders and arms, which tapered to small, almost refined hands. A mere fringe of perfectly straight black beard followed the curve of his chin, tangling itself at the ear with shaggy, unkempt locks of hair. He wore an ordinary stiff-brimmed Spanish sombrero, and the inevitable greasy red sash performed its rather difficult task of holding together flannel shirt and buckskin breeches, besides half covering with folds a long, narrow knife.

3. His companion struck me as a half-breed Indian, somewhere about eighteen years of age, his beardless face showing deep brutal lines, and a mouth which was a mere crease between hideously heavy lips. Blood stained the rowels of his spurs; an old felt hat, crumpled and ragged, slouched forward over his eyes, doing its best to hide the man. I was pleased that the stable-man who saddled Kaweah was unable to answer their inquiry where I was going, and annoyed when I heard the hotel-keeper inform them that I started next day for Millerton.

4. Leaving behind us people and village, Kaweah bore me out under the grateful shade of oaks, among rambling settlements and fields of harvested grain, whose pale-yellow stubble and stacks contrasted finely with the deep foliage, and served as a pretty groundwork for stripes of vivid green which marked the course of numberless irrigating streams. Low cottages, overarched with boughs and hemmed in with weed jungles, margined my road.

5. Trees and settlements and children were soon behind us, an open plain stretching on in front, without

visible limit. It was not pleasant to realize that I had one hundred and twenty miles of this lonely landscape ahead of me, nor that my only companion was Kaweah; for, with all his splendid powers and rare qualities of instinct, there was not the slightest evidence of response or affection in his behavior. Friendly toleration was the highest gift he bestowed on me, though I think he had great personal enjoyment in my habits as a rider.

6. The only moments that we ever seemed thoroughly *en rapport* were when I crowded him down to a wild run, using the spur and shouting at him loudly, or when, in our friendly races homeward toward camp, through the forest, I put him at a leap where he even doubted his own power. At such times I could communicate ideas to him with absolute certainty. He would stop, or turn, or gather himself for a leap at my will, as it seemed to me, by some sort of magnetic communication; but I always paid dearly for this in long, tiresome efforts to calm him. With the long, level road ahead of me, I dared not attack its monotony by any unusual riding, and, having settled him at our regular traveling trot—a gait of about six miles an hour—I forgot all about the dreary expanse of plain, and gave myself up to quiet reverie. About dusk we reached the King's River Ferry.

7. As I walked over to see Kaweah at the corral, I glanced down the river, and saw, perhaps a quarter of a mile below, two horsemen ride down one bank, spur their horses into the stream, swim to the other side, and struggle up a steep bank, disappearing among bunches of cottonwood-trees near the river. So dangerous and unusual a proceeding could not have been to save the half-dollar ferriage. There was something about their seat, and the cruel way they drove home their spurs, that, in default of better reasons, made me think them Mexicans.

8. The whole Tulare plain is the home of nomadic ranchers, who, as pasturage changes, drive about their herds of horses and cattle from range to range, and, as the wolves prowl around for prey, so a class of Mexican highwaymen rob and murder them from one year's end to another. I judged the swimmers were bent on some such errand, and lay down on the ground by Kaweah, to guard him, rolling myself in my soldier's great-coat, and slept, with saddle for a pillow. Once or twice the animal waked me by stamping restively; but I could perceive no cause for alarm, and slept on comfortably until a little before sunrise, when I rose, took a plunge in the river, and hurriedly dressed myself for the day's ride. The ferryman, who had promised to put me across the river at dawn, was already at his post, and, after permitting Kaweah to drink a deep draught, I rode him out on the ferry-boat, and was quickly at the other side.

9. The plain stretched off to my left into dusky distance, and ahead in a bare, smooth expanse, dreary by its monotony, yet not altogether repulsive in the pearly obscurity of the morning. In midsummer these plains are as hot as the Sahara through the long, blinding day; but after midnight there comes a delicious blandness upon the air, a suggestion of freshness and upspringing life, which renews vitality within you. Kaweah showed the influence of this condition in the sensitive play of ears and toss of head, and in his free, spirited stride. I was experimenting on his sensitiveness to sounds, and had found that his ears turned back at the faintest whisper, when suddenly his head rose, he looked sharply forward toward a clump of trees on the river-bank, one hundred and fifty yards in front of us, where a quick glance revealed to me a camp-fire, and two men hurrying saddles upon their horses—a gray and a sorrel.

10. They were Mexicans, the same who had swam King's River the afternoon before, and, as it flashed on me finally, the two whom I had studied so attentively at Visalia. Then I at once saw their purpose was to waylay me, and made up my mind to give them a lively run. The road followed the bank up to their camp, in an easterly direction, and then, turning a sharp right angle to the north, led out upon the open plain, leaving the river finally.

11. I decided to strike across, and threw Kaweah into a sharp trot. I glanced at my girth, and then at the bright copper upon my pistol, and settled myself firmly in the saddle. Finding that they could not saddle quickly enough to attack me mounted, the older villain grabbed a shotgun, and sprang to head me off, his comrade meantime tightening the cinches. I turned Kaweah off to the left, and tossed him a little more rein, which he understood, and sprang out into a gallop. The robber brought his gun to his shoulder, covered me, and yelled, in good English, "Hold on!"

12. At that instant his companion dashed up, leading the other horse. In another instant they were mounted and after me, yelling to the mustangs, plunging in the spurs, and shouting occasional volleys of oaths. By this time I regained the road, which lay before me, traced over the blank, objectless plain in vanishing perspective. Fifteen miles lay between me and a station; Kaweah and a pistol were my only defense; yet at that moment I felt a thrill of pleasure, a wild moment of inspiration, almost worth the danger to experience.

13. I glanced over my shoulder, and found that the Mexicans were crowding their horses to the fullest speed; their hoofs, rattling on the dry plain, were accompanied by inarticulate noises, like the cries of blood-hounds.

Kaweah comprehended the situation. I could feel his grand legs gather under me, and the iron muscles contract with excitement; he tugged at the bit, shook his bridle-chains, and flung himself impatiently into the air.

14. It flashed upon me that they had confederates concealed in some ditch far in advance of me, and that the plan was to crowd me through at the fullest speed, giving up the chase to new men and fresh horses; and I resolved to save Kaweah to the utmost, and only allow him a speed which should keep me out of gunshot. So I held him firmly, and reserved my spur for the last emergency. Still, we fairly flew over the plain, and I said to myself, as the clatter and din of my pursuers rang in my ears now and then, as the freshening breeze hurried it forward, that, if those brutes got me, there was nothing in blood and brains; for Kaweah was a prince beside their mustangs, and I ought to be worth two villains.

15. For the first twenty minutes the road was hard and smooth and level. After that gentle, shallow undulations began, and at last, at brief intervals, were sharp ditches eight or nine feet wide. I reined Kaweah in and brought him up sharply on their bottoms, giving him the bit to spring up on the other side; but he quickly taught me better, and, gathering, took them easily without my feeling it in his stride.

16. The hot sun had arisen. I saw with anxiety that the tremendous speed began to tell painfully on Kaweah. Foam tinged with blood fell from his mouth, and sweat rolled in streams from his whole body, and now and then he drew a deep-heaving breath. I leaned down and felt of the cinch to see if it had slipped forward; but as I had saddled him with great care it kept its true place, so I had only to fear the greasers behind or a new relay ahead. I was conscious of plenty of reserved speed in Kaweah,

whose powerful run was already distancing their fatigued mustangs. As we bounded down a roll of the plain, a cloud of dust sprang from a ravine directly in front of me, and two black objects lifted themselves in the sand. I drew my pistol, cocked it, whirled Kaweah to the left, plunging by and clearing by about six feet. A thrill of relief came as I saw the long white horns of Spanish cattle gleam above the dust.

17. Unconsciously I restrained Kaweah too much, and in a moment the Mexicans were crowding down upon me at a fearful rate. On they came, the crash of their spurs and the clatter of their horses distinctly heard; and as I had so often compared the beats of chronometers, I unconsciously noted that while Kaweah's, although painful, yet came with regular power, the mustangs' respiration was quick, spasmodic, and irregular. I compared the intervals of the two mustangs, and found that one breathed better than the other, and then, upon counting the best mustang with Kaweah, found that he breathed nine breaths to Kaweah's seven. In two or three minutes I tried again, finding the relation ten to seven. Then I felt the victory, and I yelled to Kaweah.

18. The thin ears shot back flat upon his neck; lower and lower he lay down to his run. I flung him a loose rein and gave him a friendly pat on the withers. It was a glorious burst of speed; the wind rushed by and the plain swept under us with dizzying swiftness. I shouted again, and the thing of nervous life under me bounded on wilder and faster, till I could feel his spine thrill as with shocks from a battery. I managed to look round—a delicate matter at speed—and saw far behind the distanced villains, both dismounted and one horse fallen.

19. In an instant I drew Kaweah into a gentle trot, looking around at every moment lest they should come on

me unawares. In a half-mile I reached the station, and I was cautiously greeted by a man who sat by the barn-door with a rifle across his knees. He had seen me come over the plain, and had also seen the Mexican horse fall. Not knowing but he might be in league with the robbers, I gave him a careful glance before dismounting, and was completely reassured by an expression of terror which had possession of his countenance.

20. I sprang to the ground and threw off the saddle, and, after a word or two with the man, who proved to be the sole occupant of this station, we fell to work upon Kaweah, my cocked pistol and his rifle lying close at hand. We sponged the creature's mouth, and, throwing a sheet over him, walked him regularly up and down for about three quarters of an hour, and then taking him upon the open plain, where we could scan the horizon in all directions, gave him a thorough grooming. I never saw him look so magnificent as when we led him down to the creek to drink. His skin was like satin, and the veins on his head and neck stood out firm and round like whipcords.

Clarence King.

CHAPTER XXI.

THE ALARM-BELL OF ATRI.

1. At Atri, in Abruzzo, a small town
 Of ancient Roman date, but scant renown—
 One of those little places that have run
 Half up the hill, beneath a blazing sun,
 And then sat down to rest, as if to say,
 "I climb no farther upward, come what may"—

The Re Giovanni, now unknown to fame,
So many monarchs since have borne the name,
Had a great bell hung in the market-place
Beneath a roof, projecting some small space,
By way of shelter from the sun and rain.
Then rode he through the streets with all his train,
And, with the blast of trumpets loud and long,
Made proclamation, that whenever wrong
Was done to any man, he should but ring
The great bell in the square, and he, the King,
Would cause the Syndic to decide thereon.
Such was the proclamation of King John.

2. How happily the days in Atri sped,
   What wrongs were righted, need not here be said.
   Suffice it that, as all things must decay,
   The hempen rope at length was worn away,
   Unraveled at the end, and, strand by strand,
   Loosened and wasted in the ringer's hand,
   Till one, who noted this in passing by,
   Mended the rope with braids of briony,
   So that the leaves and tendrils of the vine
   Hung like a votive garland at a shrine.

3. By chance it happened that in Atri dwelt
   A knight, with spur on heel and sword in belt,
   Who loved to hunt the wild boar in the woods,
   Who loved his falcons with their crimson hoods,
   Who loved his hounds and horses, and all sports
   And prodigalities of camps and courts—
   Loved, or had loved them; for at last, grown old,
   His only passion was the love of gold.

4. He sold his horses, sold his hawks and hounds,
   Rented his vineyards and his garden-grounds,

Kept but one steed, his favorite steed of all,
To starve and shiver in a naked stall,
And, day by day, sat brooding in his chair,
Devising plans how best to hoard and spare.

5. At length he said: "What is the use or need
To keep at my own cost this lazy steed,
Eating his head off in my stables here,
When rents are low and provender is dear?
Let him go feed upon the public ways;
I want him only for the holidays."
So the old steed was turned into the heat
Of the long, lonely, silent, shadowless street;
And wandered in suburban lanes forlorn,
Barked at by dogs, and torn by brier and thorn.

6. One afternoon, as in that sultry clime
It is the custom in the summer-time,
With bolted doors, and window-shutters closed,
The inhabitants of Atri slept or dozed;
When suddenly upon their senses fell
The loud alarum of the accusing bell!
The Syndic started from his sweet repose,
Turned on his couch, and listened, and then rose
And donned his robes, and with reluctant pace
Went panting forth into the market-place,
Where the great bell upon its cross-beam swung,
Reiterating with persistent tongue,
In half-articulate jargon, the old song:
"Some one hath done a wrong, hath done a wrong!"

7. But ere he reached the belfry's light arcade,
He saw, or thought he saw, beneath its shade,
No shape of human form, of woman born,
But a poor steed dejected and forlorn,

Who, with uplifted head and eager eye,
Was tugging at the vines of briony.
"Domeneddio!" cried the Syndic straight,
"This is the Knight of Atri's steed of state!
He calls for justice, being sore distressed,
And pleads his cause as loudly as the best."

8. Meanwhile from street and lane a noisy crowd
Had rolled together, like a summer cloud,
And told the story of the wretched beast
In five-and-twenty different ways at least,
With much gesticulation and appeal
To heathen gods, in their excessive zeal.
The Knight was called and questioned; in reply
Did not confess the fact, did not deny;
Treated the matter as a pleasant jest,
And set at naught the Syndic and the rest,
Maintaining, in an angry undertone,
That he should do what pleased him with his own.

9. And thereupon the Syndic gravely read
The proclamation of the King; then said:
"Pride goeth forth on horseback grand and gay,
But cometh back on foot, and begs its way;
Fame is the perfume of heroic deeds,
Of flowers of chivalry and not of weeds!
These are familiar proverbs; but I fear
They never yet have reached your knightly ear.
What fair renown, what honor, what repute
Can come to you from starving this poor brute?
He who serves well and speaks not merits more
Than they who clamor loudest at the door.
Therefore the law decrees, that as this steed
Served you in youth, henceforth you shall take heed

To comfort his old age, and to provide
Shelter in stall, and food and field beside."

10. The Knight withdrew abashed; the people all
Led home the steed in triumph to his stall.
The King heard and approved, and laughed in glee,
And cried aloud: "Right well it pleaseth me!
Church-bells at best but ring us to the door;
But go not in to mass; my bell doth more:
It cometh into court and pleads the cause
Of creatures dumb and unknown to the laws;
And this shall make, in every Christian clime,
The bell of Atri famous for all time."

Longfellow.

CHAPTER XXII.

SWINE AND THEIR FOREST COUSINS.

1. The domestic hog, has usually been regarded as a rough, stupid, and uncleanly animal. This view has been preserved in the low and unpleasant comparisons in which the pig has figured as a disgusting object. But a careful study of the nature and habits of this thick-skin, or pachyderm, shows how false is the notion. Under kind and rational treatment the pig is gentle, intelligent, and docile, and neat and orderly in its habits. The learned pig, able to distinguish letters, and perform cunning tricks, is already known to the world.

2. The intelligence of the pig is illustrated by a story preserved by the Rev. J. G. Wood. The story is told by a sailor, who describes the peculiar friendship of a pig and dog that were allowed on shipboard. The sailor says:

"The dog, you see, sir, had got a kennel for himself; the pig had nothing of the sort. We did not think he needed one; but he had notions of his own upon that matter. Why should Toby be better housed than he? Well, sir, he had somehow got it into his head that possession is nine points of the law; and, though Toby tried to show him the rights of the question, he was so pig-headed that he either would not or could not understand. So every night it came to be 'catch-as-catch-can.' If the dog got in first, he showed his teeth, and the other had to lie under the boat, or on the softest plank he could find; if the pig was found in possession, the dog could not turn him out, but looked out for his revenge next time.

3. "One evening—it had been blowing hard all day, and I had just ordered close-reefed topsails, for the gale was increasing, and there was a good deal of sea running, and it was coming on to be wet—the pig was slipping and tumbling about the decks, for the ship lay over so much with the breeze that he could not keep his hoofs. At last he thought he would secure his berth for the night, though it wanted a good bit of dusk. But lo! Toby had been of the same mind, and there he was safely housed. 'Umph! umph!' says piggy, as he turned and looked up at the sky to windward; but Toby did not offer to move. Presently he trudges off to the lee-scuppers, where the tin plate was lying from which they ate their cold potatoes. Pig takes up the plate in his mouth, and carries it to a part of the deck where the dog could see it, but some way from the kennel, then, turning his tail toward the dog, he begins to act as if he was eating out of the plate, making it rattle, and munching with his mouth pretty loud.

4. "'What!' thinks Toby, 'has piggy got victuals there?' and he pricked up his ears, and looked toward

the place, whining a little. 'Champ, champ!' goes the pig, taking not the least notice of the dog; and down goes his mouth to the plate again. Toby couldn't stand that any longer; victuals, and he not there! Out he runs, and comes up in front of the pig, with his mouth watering, and pushes his cold nose into the empty plate. Like a shot, the pig turned tail, and was snug in the kennel before Toby knew whether there was any meat or not in the plate."

The Wild Boar.

5. One can scarcely credit the fact that from the wild boar, with his rough, hideous body, savage snout, and terrible tusks, have come substantially all the finely-molded animals that mope and hobble about the better class of farms. We have large breeds and small breeds; Chester whites, Poland-Chinas, Jersey reds, Lancashires, and Berkshires, Yorkshires, Essex swine, and Suffolks. All show the purpose of the breeder in getting rid of all that is useless, long noses, ears, legs, and bodies, and retaining just what is wanted for use. So that the perfectly-bred pig looks like a brick or parallelogram in shape, has short legs, large round hams and shoulders, and plump sides. His little head and nose have just enough left to eat the carefully-prepared food that is set before him.

6. Now, if the daintily-shaped Berkshire is turned abroad into the forest to find his own living, he will begin

to grow long in legs and snout, and his progeny will rapidly degenerate toward the style of the "racers," "subsoilers," "rail-splitters," and "jumpers," that range the Western forests. It has been observed that the wild sows of the Oriental jungles keep their different litters together in a sort of corral in the woods; and when any enemy attacks them the mothers join in their defense. Our domestic pig shows the same instinct under the same circumstances.

7. "In India, boar-hunting is a favorite amusement. The hunters are always armed with javelins, which they throw at the animal as he runs away or rushes to the charge. His assaults are frequently so furious that the horses will not stand the shock, or, if they do, are often thrown down and severely injured. An instance is recorded in which a large and resolute boar, having been driven by hunters into a plain, stood at bay, challenging the whole party; he charged all horses, which advanced within fifty yards of him, with great ferocity, causing them to rear and plunge and throw their riders, whose lives were in jeopardy. Though many of the horses were accustomed to the sport, none would sustain the animal's charges, nor bring their riders within javelin-distance: at length he drove the whole party from the field, and, gnashing his teeth and foaming, he made his way to the jungle, where it was useless to pursue him further."

8. The peccary is the smallest of the original wild hogs, and it inhabits South America, Mexico, and is found in Arizona and New Mexico. "It loves forests and marshy grounds," says Mr. Jones, "but wanders wherever food may be found, sometimes committing great depredations on fields of maize or potatoes. It delights to root for bulbs, worms, or insects, but is said also to devour the eggs of birds and reptiles, and to eat of almost anything that it may find. The flesh of this animal is not very

good. The female produces but two young at a birth. These peccaries have on their back a musk-bag, from which a fetid odor is given out when the animal is excited."

9. Mr. Smith, who went to Texas in 1841, says: "The Mexican hogs (peccaries), previous to the overflow of the bottom-lands in 1833, struck terror into the hearts of the settlers in their vicinity, oftentimes pursuing the planter while hunting, or in search of the lost track of his wandering cattle, at which time they frequently killed his dogs, or even at times forced him to ascend a tree for safety, where he would sometimes be obliged to wait until the hogs got tired of dancing attendance at the foot of his place of refuge, or left him that they might go and feed.

The Peccary.

10. "These animals appeared quite savage, and would, after coming to the tree in which the planter had ensconced himself, snap their teeth and run about, and then wait for their enemy to come down. At this early period they used to hunt this animal in company: from five to fifteen planters, and occasionally a large number of hunters, would join together in the pursuit of these ravagers of their corn-fields, in order to diminish their number and prevent their further depredations, as at times they would nearly destroy a farmer's crop."

11. The wart-hog is a native of South Africa. It is

about six feet long and carries long ugly tusks, near which on each side of the snout stand out two warts or bony projections. "Hideous to a surprising extent," says Captain Harris, "but inferior in pith to his Asiatic relative, slightly built, and of very insignificant stature, his chops are armed with lancets, which in many instances attain the most astounding dimensions. The wart-hog is extremely common in the interior, where, early in the morning or at eventide, after the sun had declined, large herds were daily to be seen rooting in the open plain."

CHAPTER XXIII.

THE ARAB'S STORY OF A BOAR.

1. THE voice of the hog, usually termed grunting, is not very intelligible, nor does it convey much meaning; but the Arabs think that it speaks their own language, and that many times its speech can be understood. That this is believed is shown in the following story, told at the camp-fire by an old Reefian hunter:

2. "In the days of my youth, when a black mustache curled where now you see the hoary beard of my winter's age, I seldom passed a night within my father's hut; but, sallying out with my gun, lay in wait for the wild animals which frequented a neighboring forest. One moonlight night I had taken my position on a high rock which overhung a fountain and a small marsh—a favorable spot with our hunters to watch for boars who resorted thither to drink and root.

3. "The moon had traversed half the heavens, and I, tired with waiting, had fallen into a doze, when I was

roused by a rustling of the wood as on the approach of some large animal. I raised myself with caution, and ex-

Boar pursued by Wolves.

amined the priming of my gun ere the animal entered the marsh. He paused and seemed to be listening, when a half growl, half bark, announced him to be a boar; and a huge beast he was, and with stately step he entered the marsh.

4. "I could see by the bright moon, as he neared my station, that his bristles were white with age, and his tusks gleamed like polished steel among the dark objects around him. I cocked my gun and awaited his approach to the fountain.

5. "Having whetted his ivory tusks, he began to root;

but he appeared restless, as if he knew some enemy was at hand, for every now and then raising his snout he sniffed the air. I marveled at these movements, for as the breeze came from the quarter opposite my position, I knew I could not be an object of the boar's suspicions.

6. "Now, however, I distinctly heard a slight noise near the edge of the marsh. The boar became evidently uneasy, and I heard him say in a clear voice—for you must know they were formerly men—'I hope there is no treachery!' This he repeated once or twice, and began to root.

7. "Keeping a sharp lookout on the spot whence I heard the strange noise, I fancied I could distinguish the grim and shaggy head of a lion crouching upon his forepaws, and with eyes that glared like lighted charcoal through the bushes he seemed peering at the movements of the boar. I looked again, and now I could perceive a lion creeping cat-like on his belly as he neared the boar, who was busy rooting, but with bristles erect, and now and then muttering something I could not understand.

8. "The lion had crept within about twenty feet of the boar, but was hidden in part by some bushes. I waited breathless for the result; and although myself out of danger, I trembled with anxiety at the terrible scene that was about to take place.

9. "The boar again raised his snout and half turned his side to the lion, and I fancied I could see his eye twinkle as he watched the enemy. Another moment, and the lion made a spring, and was received by the boar, who reared upon his hind-legs. I thought I could hear the blows of his tusks as the combatants rolled upon the ground. Leaning over the rock, I strained my eyes to see the result.

10. "To my surprise the boar was again upon his legs,

and, going back a few paces, rushed at his fallen foe. A loud yell was given by the lion, which was answered by the distant howlings of the jackals. Again the ferocious boar charged till he buried his very snout in the body of the lion, who was kicking in the agonies of death. Blood, indeed, flowed from the sides of the boar, but his bristles still stood erect as he triumphed over the sultan of the forest; and now he seemed to be getting bigger and bigger. 'God is great!' said I, as I trembled with dread; 'he will soon reach me on this rock.' I threw myself flat on my face and cried out, 'There is no other God but God, and Mohammed is his prophet!'

11. "I soon recovered my courage, and looked around again. The boar had returned to his natural size and was slaking his thirst at the fountain. I seized my gun; but reflecting, said within myself: 'Why should I kill him? He will not be of any use to me; he has fought bravely and left me the skin of a lion, and perhaps he may be an evil spirit.' So I laid the gun down, contenting myself with the thought of to-morrow.

12. "The boar had left the fountain, and was again busied rooting in the marsh, when another slight noise as of a rustling in the wood attracted my notice, and I could perceive the smaller head of a lioness looking with horror at the body of her dead mate. 'God is great!' said the lioness; 'but he shall pay for it. What! a pig, an infidel! One spring, and I will do for him!' Having said these words, she advanced boldly. The boar stood prepared, grinding his teeth with rage.

13. "She paused, and again retreated to the wood; and I could hear her say: 'What an immense boar! What an infidel!'

14. "'May God burn your great-great-grandmother!' said the boar. On hearing the creature curse her parent,

she again stopped, and, lashing her tail, roared with a voice that the whole wood re-echoed; and she said, 'There is no conqueror but God!' The boar stamped his hoofs and gnashed his tusks again with rage. His grizzly bristles, red with the blood of her mate, stood on end; then, lowering his snout, he rushed headlong against the lioness, who, springing aside, avoided the dread blow.

15. "A cloud came over the moon; but I heard every blow of the paw and every rip of the tusk. There was a dead pause again. The cloud had passed and the heavens were clear, and I saw the lioness with her fore-paw on the body of the boar. I seized my gun and aimed at her head; that was her last moment.

16. "The morning dawned; I descended from the rock. The claws of the lioness still grasped in death the body of the boar. Many severe wounds showed that the boar had again fought bravely. The lions were the finest I ever saw, and I made good profit by that night's work."

CHAPTER XXIV.

GIANTS WITH TUSKS AND TRUNK.

1. THE elephant is the largest and most powerful of all living quadrupeds, and may be regarded as a remnant of those gigantic races which were common at an earlier period of the earth's history. Specimens have been found upward of twelve feet high, from the sole of the foot to the ridge of the shoulder, above five tons in weight, and capable of carrying enormous burdens. In general figure, the animal seems clumsy and awkward; but this is fully compensated by the litheness and agility of his trunk.

His legs are necessarily massive, for the support of such a huge body; but, though apparently stiff, they are by no means the unwieldy members which many suppose.

The Elephant at Work.

2. He can kneel and rise with facility; can use the fore-feet by way of hand in holding down branches while he strips off the foliage with his trunk; employ his feet in stamping his enemies to death; and has been known to travel, even with a heavy load, from fifty to seventy miles in twenty-four hours. His feet, which are internally divided into toes, are externally gathered into a round cushioned mass, protected by flattish nails, and are therefore unfitted for walking on roads or rocky ground. Less bulky in the hinder quarters, his strength accumulates in his chest and neck, the latter of which is short and well

adapted for the support of the head and trunk, which are his principal organs of action and defense.

3. Compared with the bulk of his body, the head appears small; but not so when we take into account the weight and size of its appendages. These are pendulous ears, a couple of gigantic tusks in the male, and the proboscis or trunk, which, in large specimens, is capable of reaching to a distance of seven or eight feet. The tusks, which correspond to the canine teeth of other quadrupeds, appear only in the upper jaw, fully developed in the male, and only partially in the female. These he employs as his main weapons of defense, as well as in clearing away obstructions from his path, and in grubbing up succulent roots, of which he is particularly fond. The eye of the elephant is small, but brilliant; and though, from the position in the head, it is incapable of backward and upward vision, yet this defect is remedied, to a great extent, by the acuteness of his hearing.

4. The trunk is of a tapering form, and composed of several thousand minute muscles, which cross and interlace each other, so as to give it the power of stretching and contracting, of turning itself in

1. *African Elephant.* 2. *Indian Elephant.*

every direction, and of feeling and grasping with a delicacy which is altogether astonishing. It incloses the nostrils, and has the power of inflating itself, of drawing in water, or of ejecting it with violence; it also terminates on the upper side in a sort of fleshy finger, and below in a similar protuberance, which answers to the opposing power of the thumb, and thus it can lift the minutest object.

5. Endowed with exquisite sensibility, nearly eight feet in length, and stout in proportion to the massive size of the whole animal, this organ, at the volition of the elephant, will uproot trees or gather grass, raise a piece of artillery or pick up a comfit, kill a man or brush off a fly. It conveys the food to the mouth, and pumps up the enormous draughts of water, which, by its recurvature, are turned into and driven down the capacious throat or showered over the body. Its length supplies the place of a long neck, which would have been incompatible with the support of the large head and weighty tusks of the animal.

6. The elephant is a pachyderm, and its skin, like that of the horse, is extremely sensitive, so that it feels the attacks of the tiniest insects; hence he takes care to syringe it with his trunk, cover it with dust and saliva, or fan it with a leafy bough. The skin has muscles attached to it, so that the elephant, like the horse, can, by a sort of quivering motion, shake off flies and loose particles of dust.

7. In its mode of life the elephant is strictly herbivorous, feeding upon grass, young shoots of trees, and succulent roots. His whole conformation is eminently for such subsistence, and points to the tropical valley and fertile river-side as the localities where he can enjoy, at all seasons, herbage and water in abundance. Though created for the jungle and forest, where heat and moisture are the chief vegetative agents, yet the elephant, by his weight and size, is excluded from the swamp. He bathes in the river and lake only where the bottom is firm and secure, and rolls on the sward or in the forest glade. Confined to

the regions of an almost perpetual summer, he grubs up roots with his tusks, pulls down branches with his trunk to browse on their foliage, or feeds on the luxuriant herbage, enjoying greater ease and security than any

The Elephant and the Tiger.

other quadruped. His great size and strength place him beyond the dread of other animals; and, like all the herbivora, he is of mild disposition, having no occasion to wage war upon others for the satisfaction of his natural cravings.

8. The home of the wild elephant is in Central and Southern Africa and in India. The most effective way of capturing them is by means of inclosures, into which a herd is driven and kept until tamed. In preparing for the drives of a large herd, the hunters, numbering from

two to five hundred, proceed to the region where the wild elephants are known to be. Here, in some convenient place, they form an inclosure, which consists of a deep ditch or a strong palisade of timber. The elephant has a mortal fear of a ditch, and, when it encounters one, it will follow along its bank for miles rather than attempt to cross it. Where the ground is not favorable for digging, a barricade of posts and logs is erected. This inclosure is quite extensive, and has within it a number of large trees. The opening into this space is narrow, and the avenue leading to it has converging lines of ditches and barricades, which at their outer angle are wide apart.

9. The wild elephants in the jungle are then carefully surrounded by the hunters, and by skillful and judicious handling are gradually driven toward the entrance of the pen. When once surrounded, great fires are kept up on the opposite side to keep them from breaking out and escaping. If the herd is large, it may take several days to bring them within the entrance of the inclosure. The hunters then rapidly close in upon them, and, as all danger seems to be in the rear, they press forward through the narrow entrance, which is immediately closed by dropping a strong portcullis from above. The elephants thus entrapped are then approached by the aid of tame elephants, and secured by fastening ropes around their legs and tying them to trees. By skillful and kindly handling the wild elephants become tame in the course of one or two weeks.

10. Elephants are trained to do a great many different kinds of work. "To give an idea of these labors," says Bingley, "it is sufficient to remark that all the tuns, sacks, and bales transported from one place to another in India, are carried by elephants; that they carry burdens on their bodies, their necks, their tusks, and even in their mouths,

by giving them the end of a rope, which they hold fast in their teeth; that, uniting sagacity to strength, they never break anything committed to their charge; that from the banks of the rivers they put their bundles into boats, without wetting them, laying them down gently, and arranging them where they ought to be placed; that when disposed in the places where their masters direct, they try with their trunks whether the goods are properly stowed; and, if a tun or cask rolls, they go of their own accord in quest of stones to prop and render it firm."

11. The elephant is intelligent and sagacious, and on occasions can do many extraordinary things. It readily obeys its keeper, and, if treated kindly, has a strong affection for him. For so large an animal, it is timid, and its submission to man has an element of fear as well as love. It is subject to fits of rage, when no one is safe within its reach. Innumerable stories are told illustrative of the intelligence, gratitude, memory, resentment, and attachment of elephants. We have room for only one. "An elephant in Ajmeer, which frequently passed through the bazaar, or market, as he went by a certain herb-woman always received from her a mouthful of greens. At length he was seized with one of his periodical fits of rage, broke from his fetters, and, running through the market, put the crowd to flight, and among others this woman, who in her haste forgot a little child she had brought with her. The animal, gratefully recollecting the spot where his benefactress was wont to sit, laid aside his fury, and, taking up the infant gently in his trunk, placed it in safety on a stall before a neighboring house."

12. The tapir, a distant cousin of the elephant, inhabits the tropical forests of South America, and the Malayan Peninsula of Asia. It is about as large as a donkey of moderate size, and it is provided with a movable probos-

cis, something between the trunk of an elephant and the snout of a hog. It is omnivorous, but it feeds principally

The Tapir.

upon the tender leaves and stalks of plants—coming out at night, and sleeping during the greater part of the day. In form and structure it is like the hog, and, also like that animal, it delights to wallow in the mud. It has formidable teeth for defense, great powers of swimming, and, with its head as a wedge, it can easily penetrate dense jungles, its thick hide protecting it from injury. Prepared in this way for fight or flight, it meets but few enemies from which it can not escape. In disposition the tapir is like the elephant, and is easily tamed.

CHAPTER XXV.

THE MONARCH OF AFRICAN WATERS.

1. On the 5th of November, 1604, the whole of London was in a state of commotion at hearing of the discovery of "Guy Fawkes" sitting in a cellar under the Houses of Parliament, on a powder-barrel, with a match in his hand, his intention being to blow up James I and the House of Lords. On the 5th of November, 1872, two hundred and sixty-eight years later, London was again put in a state of commotion by the appearance of another "Guy Fawkes"; this time, however, not in the cellar under the Houses of Parliament, but in the straw by the side of his mother, in her den at the Zoölogical Gardens. This celebrated animal, "Guy Fawkes," is so called on account of the date of his birth.

2. A few days after the birth of the young one, Mr Bartlett was watching it swimming about the tank. It

The Hippopotamus.

then suddenly dived, but did not reappear for such a long time, that he thought it had had a fit, and was lying drowned at the bottom of the tank. He therefore made arrangements to have the large plug pulled out—this plug had been expressly fixed for this purpose—and to run off the tank quickly, so as to resuscitate the little beast, if possible. They were just going to do this, when Master "Guy Fawkes" suddenly reappeared, shaking his funny little horse-like ears, from the bottom of his tank, with a hippopotamic grin on his face, as much as to say: "Don't be frightened, I am all right; you don't know all about me yet." The little beast had remained, without blowing or taking breath, actually under water for nearly twenty minutes. The parents have never been known to be under water much over three minutes.

3. I suspect Nature has given this wonderful power of remaining so long under water to the young hippopotamus, first of all, to enable it to suck—when the water has been clear, Mr. Bartlett has frequently seen it sucking under water; and, secondly, in order that it may be concealed from its enemies, though I am not at all certain but that a large crocodile would seize and swallow a young hippopotamus, as a jack would swallow a roach.

4. Master Guy Fawkes, nevertheless, had one day a narrow escape of his life. In order to clean out the tank, one fine, sunny morning, the mother and child were let out into the pond outside. They both remained in the water as long as it suited them, and then the mother walked out, with that peculiar stately gait which distinguishes this gigantic animal. The little one attempted to follow, but, unfortunately, he chose a landing-place at the corner nearest the giraffe's inclosure, just at the very point where there were no steps. The poor little fellow struggled hard to get out, but could not, falling back into the water.

5. His mother, seeing the distress of her child, immediately went back into the water, and, diving down, brought him up from the bottom. She then supported his head above the water, in order to give him time to breathe. For nearly half an hour Mr. Bartlett and the keepers were in agonies. Of course, they dared not go to help Guy Fawkes, and there was no form of life-buoy they could throw to the struggling creature. At last the young one made a more vigorous effort than ever, when simultaneously the old one gave him a push with her tremendous head, and the little animal's life was thus saved. So we see that the hippopotamus is no fool; her instinct —mind, rather—told her how to save her young one.

6. This little animal is about the size and shape of an ordinary bacon-pig, but the color is something of a pinkish-slate. He knows his keeper very well; and, when he has had his dinner, is as playful as a kitten, popping and jumping about his den, and throwing up mouthfuls of hay like a young calf. When first born, he was small enough to come through the bars on to the straw outside his den, but soon he had grown so much that he could not get through. He used to put his head through the bars, and allow Prescott, the keeper, to rub his gums.

7. I now proceed to make some general remarks about hippopotami. The hippopotamus is of some value commercially. The skin is made by the natives into whips, which, I believe, are used to beat delinquents in Egypt; and I am told that they are exceedingly formidable weapons. To make the whip, the skin is cut into slips, about five or six feet long, one end being pointed, the other broad; it is then coiled upon itself, and afterward dried in the sun; and, when finished, is light, dry, and elastic. The teeth of the hippopotamus are also of commercial value.

8. Their structure is very peculiar. I have a tooth

now before me; it is hollow at one end, like the tusk of an elephant. When the animal was alive, this hollow was filled with soft pulp. The tooth is always growing forward as the pulp solidifies behind. The reader can easily see how this is, by examining the front tooth of the lower jaw of the next boiled rabbit he has for dinner. The outside of the tooth of the hippopotamus is formed of a glass-like, hard enamel; it is exceedingly dense, hard, and flint-like. I have just taken down my old regimental sword, and find that, by striking it at the proper angle, a shower of sparks fly away from the tooth, like the sparks from a boy's "fire-devil," made in form of a pyramid with wet gunpowder. The teeth of the hippopotami, as in the rabbit, are sometimes liable to deformity. In the College of Surgeons there is the tooth of a hippopotamus which has grown nearly into the form of a circle.

9. Not long ago the old male hippopotamus at the Gardens suffered from a decayed tooth. Mr. Bartlett, with his ever-ready talent in meeting all emergencies, determined to pull out the tooth. He ordered the blacksmith to make a pair of "tooth-forceps," and a tremendous pair they were. The "bite" of the forceps just fitted the tooth of the hippo. By skillful management, Bartlett contrived to seize Master Hippo's tooth, as he put his head through the bars. The hippo, roaring frightfully, pulled one way, Bartlett and the keepers pulled the other, and at last out came the tooth, and hippo soon got well again.

10. No animal in the world is made without purpose, and we always find that the structure of an animal is admirably adapted to its mode of life. I believe that one of the principal duties which the elephant and rhinoceros unconsciously perform is to cut paths through the dense forest and jungles in which they live. The home of the

hippopotamus is among the aquatic forests at the bottoms of large rivers, such as the upper Nile. It is probable that, in the days of Moses, these animals abounded in Lower Egypt. I believe they do not now occur in any part of the Nile below the cataracts, the headquarters being the central and southern parts of Africa only; but I am afraid that, as civilization increases, so will the hippopotamus retreat.

11. This huge animal spends most of its time in the water, and it comes out to feed at night. Above the cataracts of the Nile they are very destructive to crops, as they eat an immense quantity, and trample down much more than they eat. The stomach contains as much as five or six bushels, and the large intestine is eight inches in diameter. They do not grind their food much, but rather munch it up. The reader should be curious to notice this at the Zoölogical Gardens. When the old hippo opens its mouth, a good-sized baby could as easily be put in as one puts a letter into a letter-box. As the elephant makes passes in the jungles, so it appears to me that one of the chief offices of the hippopotamus is to keep in check the dense vegetation in tropical climates, which, if allowed to accumulate, would block up the long reaches of rivers, and ultimately turn the flat lands into useless, fever-breeding swamps; so that we see that this gigantic animal is of very considerable economic importance.

12. This living machine for the destruction of fresh-water vegetation is admirably adapted to its work. Nature has not given him any hair, as that would be an incumbrance to him, and would not well conduce to his comfort when wallowing in the mud. The skin is, therefore, somewhat like that of a pig. If the animal had not some protection against the sudden changes of temperature, induced by his going in and out of the water so frequently,

he would always be either shivering or else unbearably hot. Nature, therefore, has given him a thick layer of fat between the skin and the muscles.

13. In the water the hippopotamus, though a gigantic beast, shows very little of his carcass. On referring to the engraving, it will be observed that the nostrils, eyes, and ears are on the same level. The nostrils are each provided with a wonderful valve, by means of which he can open his nostrils to breathe, or shut them up to exclude the water. This beautiful mechanism is worked by what is called a "sphincter-muscle." Reader, your own eyes are worked by a sphincter-muscle. Stand opposite the looking-glass and wink at yourself; you will then see a sphincter-muscle in operation.

14. You do not require a sphincter-muscle to your nose, because you are not amphibious. We find, however, that the seal, like the hippopotamus, can close his nose at will by a sphincter-muscle. Go and look at the seal in the Zoölogical Garden. The valve which works the blow-hole of the whale and porpoise is of an analogous character. Strange to say, we find an animal that is not amphibious which has his nostrils protected by this curious and beautiful valve. But you will, probably, never guess what that animal is. Well, it is the camel—the "ship of the desert." In the desert, where the camel lives, there are often "sand-storms," and the Creator has provided the poor camel with this wonderful structure, to save him from suffocation when these terrible sand-storms occur.

Frank Buckland.

CHAPTER XXVI.

THE GIANT PIG OF THE JUNGLE.

1. BEARING in mind that the rhinoceros of Asia has one horn, and that of Africa has two horns, we can scarcely find a more spirited or complete description of this ugly beast than that given by Hartwig, in his "Tropical World": "The rhinoceros," he says, "has about the same range as the elephant, but is found also in the Island of Java, where the latter is unknown. Although not possessed of the

The Rhinoceros and its Neighbors.

ferocity of carnivorous animals, this pachyderm is completely wild and untamable; the image of a gigantic hog, without intelligence, feeling, or docility, and, though emulating the elephant in size, is infinitely inferior in point of sagacity. The latter, with his beautiful, intelligent eye, awakens the sympathy of man; while the rhinoceros is the very image of brutal violence and stupidity.

2. "It was formerly supposed that Africa had but one rhinoceros; but the researches of modern travelers have discovered no less than four different species, two white and two black, each of them with two horns. In both species the upper lip projects over the lower, and is capable of being extended like that of the giraffe, thus enabling the animal to grasp the branches on whose foliage he intends to feed. The black species are extremely ill-natured, and, with the exception of the buffalo, are the most dangerous of all the animals of South Africa. The white species are distinguished by one of the horns attaining the prodigious length of four feet.

3. "Although the black and white rhinoceroses are members of the same family, their mode of living and disposition are totally different. The food of the former consists almost entirely of roots, which they dig up with their larger horn, or of the branches and sprouts of the thorny acacia; while the latter live exclusively on grasses. Perhaps in consequence of their milder food they are of a timid, unsuspecting nature, which renders them an easy prey, so that they are fast melting away before the march of the European trader; while the black species, from their greater ferocity and wariness, maintain their place much longer than their more timid relations. The flesh of the black rhinoceros has a bitter taste, and, like the generality of ill-natured animals, not an ounce of fat on the bones; while that of the white species is juicy and well-flavored.

4. "The shape of the rhinoceros is unwieldy and

massive; its vast paunch hangs down nearly to the ground; its short legs are strong, like columns, and have three toes on each foot; the misshapen head has long and erect ears, and ludicrously small eyes; the skin, which is completely naked, with the exception of some coarse bristles at the tail and the upper end of the ears, is comparatively smooth in the African species, but extremely rough in the Asiatic, hanging in large folds about the animal, like a mantle. From the snout to the tip of the tail the African rhinoceros attains a length of from fifteen to sixteen feet, a girth of from ten to twelve feet, and a weight of from four thousand to five thousand pounds; but, in spite of its ponderous and clumsy proportions, it is able to speed like lightning, particularly when pursued. It then seeks the nearest wood, and dashes with all its might through the thicket.

5. "The rhinoceros is endowed with an extraordinary acuteness of smell and hearing; he listens with attention to every sound, and is able to scent from a great distance the approach of man; but, as the range of his small, deep-set eyes is impeded by his unwieldy horns, he can only see what is immediately before him, so that if one be to leeward of him it is not difficult to approach within a few paces. To make up for the imperfection of its sight, it is frequently accompanied by a beautiful green-backed and blue-winged bird, about the size of a jay, who warns it of approaching danger by its cry.

6. "'Many a time,' says Gordon Cumming, 'have these watchful attendants disappointed me in my stalk. They are the best friends the rhinoceros has, and rarely fail to awaken him, even in his soundest nap. He perfectly understands their warning, and, springing to his feet, he generally first looks about him in every direction, after which he invariably makes off. I have often hunted

a rhinoceros on horseback, which led me a chase of many miles, and required a number of shots before he fell, during which chase several of these birds remained with their ugly friend to the last.

7. "'They reminded me of mariners on the deck of some bark, sailing on the ocean, for they perched along his back and sides, and, as each of my bullets told on the shoulder of the rhinoceros, they ascended about six feet into the air, uttering their harsh cry of alarm, and then resumed their position. It sometimes happened that the lower branches of trees under which the rhinoceros passed swept them from their living deck, but they always recovered their former station; they also adhere to the rhinoceros during the night. I have often shot these animals at midnight, when drinking at the fountains, and the birds, imagining they were asleep, remained with them till morning, and on my approaching, before taking flight, they exerted themselves to their utmost to awaken the rhinoceros from his deep sleep.'

8. "The black rhinoceroses are of a gloomy, melancholy temper, and not seldom fall into paroxysms of rage without any evident cause, often plowing up the ground for several yards with their horns, and assaulting large bushes in the most violent manner. Seeing the creatures in their wild haunts cropping the bushes, or quietly moving through the plains, you might take them for the most inoffensive animals in all Africa; but, when roused to passion, there is nothing more terrific on earth. All the beasts of the wilderness are afraid of him. The lion silently retires from his path, and even the elephant is glad to get out of his way. Yet this brutal and stupidly hoggish animal is distinguished by its parental love, and the tenderness which it bestows on its young is returned with equal affection.

9. "As is the case with many other tropical animals, the huge beast awakens to a more active life after sunset. It then hastens to the lake or river to slake its thirst, or to wallow in the mud, thus covering its hide with a thick coat of clay against the attacks of flies. During the night it rambles over a great extent of country, but soon after sunrise seeks shelter against the heat under the shade of a tree or rock, where it spends the greater part of the day in sleep, either stretched at full length or in a standing position. Thus seen from a distance it might easily be mistaken for a huge block of stone.

10. "From what has been related of the fury of the rhinoceros, its pursuit must be attended with considerable danger, and thus the annals of the wild sports of Southern Africa are full of hair-breadth escapes from its terrific charge. Once Mr. Oswell, having lodged a ball in the body of a huge white rhinoceros, was surprised to see the beast, instead of seeking safety in flight, as is generally the case with this inoffensive species, suddenly stop short, and, having eyed him curiously for a second or two, walk slowly toward him. Though never dreaming of danger, he instinctively turned his horse's head away; but, strange to say, this creature, usually so docile, now absolutely refused to give him his head.

11. "When at last he did so it was too late, for, although the rhinoceros had only been walking, the distance was now so small that contact was unavoidable. In another moment the brute bent low his head, and, with a thrust upward, struck his horn into the ribs of the horse with such force as to penetrate to the very saddle on the opposite side, when the rider felt its sharp point against his leg. The violence of the blow was so tremendous as to cause the horse to make a complete somersault in the air, coming down heavily on his back.

12. "The rider was, of course, violently precipitated to the ground. While thus prostrated he saw the horn of the monster alongside of him; but, without attempting to do any further mischief, the brute started off at a canter from the scene of action. If the rhinoceros imagined it had come off victor, it was soon undeceived, for Mr. Oswell, rushing upon one of his companions, who by this time had come up, and, unceremoniously pulling him off his horse, leaped into the saddle, and, without a hat, his face streaming with blood, was quickly in pursuit of the beast, which he soon had the satisfaction to see stretched lifeless at his feet."

13. In the rhinoceros and the hippopotamus we see interesting links in the chain which holds together the great kingdom of animals. The hippopotamus, living both in the water and on the land, and, by its peculiar toes, bears a resemblance to the walrus and seal of the cetacean group on the one hand, and points to the pig and larger herb-eating animals on the other. The rhinoceros, in its general character and in its three cetacean toes, looks toward the hippopotamus on the one side, and, in its life on the land and its way of feeding, to the higher animals of the land on the other.

CHAPTER XXVII.

THE FIFTIETH BIRTHDAY OF AGASSIZ.

1. It was fifty years ago,
  In the pleasant month of May,
  In the beautiful Pays de Vaud,
  A child in its cradle lay.

2. And Nature, the old nurse, took
   The child upon her knee,
Saying, "Here is a story-book
   Thy Father has written for thee."

3. "Come, wander with me," she said,
   "Into regions yet untrod;
And read what is still unread
   In the manuscripts of God."

4. And he wandered away and away
   With Nature, the dear old nurse,
Who sang to him night and day
   The rhymes of the universe.

5. And whenever the way seemed long,
   Or his heart began to fail,
She would sing a more wonderful song
   Or tell a more marvelous tale.

6. So she keeps him still a child,
   And will not let him go,
Though at times his heart beats wild
   For the beautiful Pays de Vaud;

7. Though at times he hears in his dreams
   The Ranz des Vaches of old,
And the rush of mountain streams
   From glaciers clear and cold;

8. And the mother at home says, "Hark!
   For his voice I listen and yearn;
It is growing late and dark,
   And my boy does not return."

Longfellow.

CHAPTER XXVIII.

OUR FARM-YARD MILK-GIVERS.

" In the furrowed land
The toilsome and patient oxen stand;
Lifting the yoke-encumbered head,
With their dilated nostrils spread,
They silently inhale
The clover-scented gale,
And the vapors that arise
From the well-watered and smoking soil.
For this rest in the furrow after toil
Their large and lustrous eyes
Seem to thank the Lord
More than man's spoken word."

1. WE owe a debt of gratitude to the poets who, like Longfellow in these graphic lines, have preserved to us pictures of animal life now rapidly passing out of fact. The time has been when the farm scene was incomplete without the patient oxen laboring before their load, resting in the furrow, or reposing in the shade chewing their comforting cud, and looking out of soft brown eyes. Now the ox is scarcely to be seen, except as a grazer in the herd or hanging in the butcher's stall. His place is supplied by the horse, or by the long-eared, nimble-footed prosy mule; the cow remains. Her golden products still shine on the farmer's table, and she sends her influence into crowded cities in the form of mild, diluent, and harmless fluid.

2. To write the history of the ox or cow is to trace the history of man. Who first caught and tamed the wild beasts that were the original parents of our domestic cattle we shall never know. Egyptians, Assyrians, Hebrews, Greeks, Gauls, and Britons, all had cattle for the yoke

and the pail. Everywhere and in all ages this animal has been an indispensable servant of man's home and life.

Beside the Woodland Pool.

It has given him a back for burdens, a shoulder for power, meat and milk for food, leather for clothing, and horn, glue, and hair for other necessary uses.

3. Under the influence of different climates, uses,

treatments, and selection continued for many ages, cattle have assumed several distinct types called breeds. These breeds show certain characteristics that have become definite and fixed by time, and by the different uses or purposes that have controlled their selection. Where broad plains encouraged the raising of beef, the mind and hand of man have selected for propagation in each generation those animals only that were best adapted for this purpose. In the same manner where broken surfaces favored the production of milk, there the best milkers were reserved from each generation, and so on until the purpose of man became fixed in the main features of the animal.

4. Our native cattle represent the varied wants and indefinite purposes of a newly-settled country and a mixed people. They are the result of original stock imported from nearly every quarter of the globe, and they have not been bred to any one special use. They are, therefore, of all

Hungarian Oxen.

shapes and colors, with and without horns, and have been equally serviceable for the yoke, for beef, milk, butter, and cheese. The distinct breeds of cattle that have been introduced to satisfy the wants of advanced agriculture may be divided into two general classes—the one excellent for beef, and the other for milk and its products. Each of these classes, however, serves to some extent the purposes of the other; the beef class is used for milk, and the milk class for beef. The beef breeds best known among us are the Devon, Durham, or Short-horn, the Hereford, and the Polled Angus. The milk breeds embrace the Ayrshire, Jersey, or Alderney, the Guernsey, the Holstein, and the Swiss.

5. The Devons, closely and carefully bred for centuries in Devonshire, England, are of medium size, compact, of deep-red color, with white graceful horns. They are docile, active, surpass all others for the yoke, while many individuals and strains are excellent milkers and butter-makers. The Durhams, or Short-horns, take their name from the county of the same name in the north of England, where they are most extensively raised. They are supposed to have originated on the Continent. They are the ideal beef breed, showing an almost parallelogram in the shape of their bodies. Of mixed red and white—roan —or solid red colors, with short crumpled horns and fine muzzle, they are the aristocrats of cattle, the pets of lords, and the pride of stock raisers.

6. The Herefords, from Herefordshire, in England, recognized by their deep-red body color, with white face, white-lined backs, and horns of medium length, are larger than the Devons, often reaching the weight of Short-horns, and are active, hardy, and easily fattened. Very similar to the other beef breeds in its tendency to take flesh is the Polled Angus, jet-black and without horns.

7. The Ayrshire among milk breeds is the pride of the Scotch farmer and dairyman. She is party-colored, red and white, with horns of medium length, and deep, broad body. In her native home she is prized above all others for butter, cheese, and milk. In this country she is distinguished as a cheese cow, and excels in the quantity of milk. Coming from her home in Holland, the Holstein stands at the head of milk-givers. She is at once recognized by her large, bony frame set upon long legs, her patches of black and white color, her long slim neck, crumpled horns, and intelligent face. Her capacity for milk is enormous. Her milk is of good quality, and she is profitable for beef when her milking period is past.

8. The Channel Island cattle, from the Islands of Alderney, Jersey, and Guernsey, are of Norman extraction. The original importation to this country was probably from Alderney. The most distinct type and style, bred and fixed by ages of careful selection and legal protection, comes from the larger Island of Jersey. By far the largest proportion of this class has come from Jersey, and this name is recognized as proper to the race. The Jerseys are comparatively small, bony, of reddish-brown, bronze, fawn, or squirrel color, either solid or party-colored with white, usually of orange dyed skin, small neck and head, with prominent black eyes and crumpled horns, and a peculiar fillet about the eyes and nose. The Jersey's nature is adapted to produce rich milk and golden butter. She is averse to flesh, and on this account is not profitable for beef.

9. A larger cow, and not so delicate in form as the Jersey, is the Guernsey, from a neighboring island of the same name. She is party-colored, light red and white, gives a larger quantity of milk than the Jersey, and produces butter of a deeper orange-color. She is also profit-

able for beef when useless for milk. The practical farmer and dairyman secure the main benefits of these fixed types of cattle by a mixture of their blood with that of the native stock. The home cow is called "our royal divinity" by Mr. John Burroughs, whose pleasant sketch is here partly given:

10. "What a variety of individualities a herd of cows presents when you have come to know them all, not only in form and color, but in manners and disposition! Some are timid and awkward, and the butt of the whole herd; some remind you of deer; some have an expression in the face like certain persons you have known. A petted, well-fed cow has a benevolent and gracious look; an ill-used and poorly-fed one a pitiful and forlorn look. Some cows have a masculine or ox expression; others are extremely feminine. The latter are the ones for milk. Some cows will kick like a horse; some jump fences like a deer. Every herd has its ringleader, its unruly spirit—one that plans all the mischief and leads the rest through the fences into the grain or into the orchard. This one is usually quite different from the master-spirit, the 'boss of the yard.' The latter is generally the most peaceful and law-abiding cow in the lot, and the least bullying and quarrelsome.

11. "But she is not to be trifled with—her will is law; the whole herd give way to her, those that have crossed horns with her, and those that have not, but yielded their allegiance without crossing. I remember such a one among my father's milkers when I was a boy—a slender-horned, deep-shouldered, large-uddered, dewlapped old cow that we always put first in the long stable, so she could not have a cow on each side of her to forage upon; for the master is yielded to no less in the stanchions than in the yard. She always had the first place anywhere.

She had her choice of standing-room, in the milking-yard, and when she wanted to lie down there, or in the fields, the best and softest spot was hers.

12. "When the herd were foddered from the stack or barn, or fed with pumpkins in the fall, she was always first served. Her demeanor was quiet, but impressive. She never bullied or gored her mates, but literally ruled them with the breath of her nostrils. If any new-comer or ambitious younger cow, however, chafed under her supremacy, she was ever ready to make good her claims. And with what spirit would she fight when openly challenged! She was a whirlwind of pluck and valor; and not after one defeat or two defeats would she yield the championship. The boss-cow, when overcome, seems to brood over her disgrace, and day after day will meet her rival in fierce combat.

13. "A friend of mine, a pastoral philosopher, whom I have consulted in regard to the master-cow, thinks it is seldom the case that one rules all the herd, if it number many, but that there is often one that will rule nearly all. 'Curiously enough,' he says, 'a case like this will often occur: No. 1 will whip No. 2; No. 2 whips No. 3, and No. 3 whips No. 1; so around in a circle. This is not a mistake; it is often the case. I remember,' he continued, 'we once had feeding out of a large bin, in the center of the yard, six oxen who mastered right through in succession from No. 1 to No. 6; but No. 6 paid off the score by whipping No. 1.'

14. "How wise and sagacious the cows become that run upon the street, or pick their living along the highway! The mystery of gates and bars is at last solved to them. They ponder over them by night, they lurk about them by day, till they acquire a new sense—till they become *en rapport* with them and know when they are open

and unguarded. The garden-gate, if it open into the highway at any point, is never out of the mind of these roadsters, or out of their calculations. They calculate upon the chances of its being left open a certain number of times in the season; and if it be but once, and only for five minutes, your cabbage and sweet-corn suffer.

15. "What villager, or countryman either, has not been awakened at night by the squeaking and crunching of those piratical jaws under the window or in the direction of the vegetable-patch? I have had the cows, after they had eaten up my garden, break into the stable where my own milcher was tied, and gore her and devour her meal. Yes, life presents but one absorbing problem to the street-cow, and that is how to get into your garden."

CHAPTER XXIX.

THE BOVINE DWELLERS OF OTHER LANDS.

1. It will be observed, in looking at the pictures of buffalo and bison, that there is a striking difference between these two animals. There are but two species of buffalo; one is a native of India, the other of South Africa. The buffalo is a rougher animal than our domestic ox, yet in general form much like the ox. His peculiarities lie mainly in the shape of the head and horns. The top of his head is round or convex, and his horns curve downward, outward, and upward. The bison, on the other hand, has a singular hump over the shoulders, covered by a shaggy mane, a rounded head, and a short, upright curved horn. The name buffalo was long ago given to the Indian and African species, and, as will be seen, can

not properly apply to the so-called buffalo of America, which is a true bison.

2. The Indian buffalo, or arna, as it is called, is, in its wild state, ten feet long and six feet high, and wears a coat of smooth, thin, short hair. It frequents the great swampy jungles of India, and is fierce and pugnacious in disposition. It wallows in the mud, and seems to prefer the lower and more unfrequented lands. Here it sometimes comes in conflict with the Bengal tiger, for whom it is more than a match. But this buffalo has been tamed in its native land, and applied to practical use. During the middle ages it was introduced into Egypt, Greece, and Italy. Its great strength adapts it to the yoke; its milk is good, but its flesh is not pleasant. The Cape buffalo of

A Buffalo Cow defending her Calf.

South Africa is neither so high nor so large as its Indian cousin, but it is equally ferocious, and does not wait for a provocation, but wages a wanton war on men and animals. It collects in great herds, and delights to wallow in the mire.

3. The European bison, or ure-ox, is one of the largest of terrestrial mammals. It coexisted with the extinct mammoth, and would have been swept out of existence long ago but for the order of the Emperor of Russia against its destruction. The American bison, commonly called buffalo, needs no description. Its story has often been written. It is an inmate of the zoölogical gardens, and an *attaché* of the common showman. Though it wears a fierce and menacing look, it never attacks man. But when the long procession of buffaloes starts for the distant watering-place, and the black column moves with dashing power across the plain, then both the man and the railway-train must clear the track.

4. Mr. Ernest Ingersoll, in "The Popular Science Monthly," says of this animal: "As is well known, the buffalo is pre-eminently gregarious — herds numbering millions of individuals, and blackening the whole landscape, having formerly been met with on the plains. Emigrant-trains used to be delayed by the passing of dense herds, and during the first years of the Kansas-Pacific Railway its trains were frequently stopped by the same cause. These masses seem to have some sort of organization, consisting of small bands which unite in migration or when pursued, but separate when feeding. The cows with their calves and the younger animals are generally toward the middle of the small herd, while the older bulls are found on the outside, and the patriarchs of the herd bring up the rear. The real guardians are the vigilant cows, who usually lead the movements of the herd.

5. "The behavior of buffaloes is very much like that of domestic cattle, but their speed and endurance seem to be far greater. When well under way, it takes a fleet horse to overtake them; and they raise a column of dust, which

marks their progress when far away. They swim rivers with ease, even amid floating ice, and show a surprising agility and expertness in making their way down precipitous cliffs and banks of streams, plunging headlong where a man would pick his way with hesitation. Ordinarily, however, the buffalo exhibits commendable sagacity in his choice of routes, usually taking the easiest grades and the most direct course, so that a buffalo-trail—often worn deep into the ground—can be depended on as affording the most feasible road through the region it traverses.

6. "When belligerent, the old bulls make the most blustering demonstrations, but are really cowardly. Facing the approaching hunter with a boastful and defiant

The Bison Hunt.

air, they will pace to and fro, threateningly pawing the earth, only to take to their heels the next moment. The bulls greatly enjoy pawing the earth, and throwing it up with their horns, digging into banks, or getting down on one knee to strike into the level surface, so that the sheaths of their horns are always badly splintered. They are very fond, too, of rubbing themselves, and evidently regard the telegraph-poles along the railroads as set there for their especial convenience in this respect.

7. "But their chief delight is in wallowing. Finding in the low parts of the prairie a little stagnant water among the grass, or, at least, the surface soft and moist, an old bull plunges his horns into the ground, tearing up the earth, and soon making an excavation into which the water trickles, forming for a short time a cool and comfortable bath, in which he wallows, like a hog in the mire, swinging himself round and round on his side, and thus enlarging the pool until he is nearly immersed. At length he rises besmeared with a coating of mud, which, drying, insures him immunity from pests for many hours. Others follow, each enlarging the 'wallow,' until it becomes twenty feet in diameter, remains a prominent feature in the landscape, and forms a cistern where a grateful supply of water is often long retained for the thirsty denizens of that dry region."

The Zebu.

8. The zebus are the domestic cattle of India, and are also found in China and in some parts of Africa. Some of them are as large as our native cattle, and others are as small as a yearling calf. They have a peculiar hump on their shoulders, and are covered with a soft, mouse-colored or squirrel-gray hair. The natives are taught by their religion that it is a sin to kill these cattle; hence they are named sacred cattle. They are useful for the saddle, for drawing carriages, and are sometimes attached to the plow. Their step is rapid, and they can easily travel

thirty miles in a day. They are managed by a small cord passed through the gristle of the nose. Their flesh is esteemed by Europeans as an article of food.

9. "An old writer describes the procession of an Indian prince, who was drawn by two white oxen, which had the neck short, and a hump between the shoulders, but which were as lively and active as horses. Bishop Heber informs us that the horns of the white oxen which drag the Rajpoot nobility are gilded. It is said that they can travel fifty miles a day, and always on a trot. When they have done half their day's work, they have for dinner two or three balls of the size of a penny loaf, and made of wheaten flour, kneaded with butter and coarse sugar; and, in the evening, their supper consists of chick-peas, bruised and steeped for half an hour in water."

The Yak of Thibet.

10. "The yak, or grunting cow, is distinguished from the true oxen by its smaller stature, by the long hair that

clothes its body, and by a kind of mane that runs along the center of its back and shoulders, as well as by the peculiarity of the sounds to which it gives utterance. The yak is a native of Thibet, inhabiting the loftiest plateaux of high Asia." Dr. Hooker further describes it: "The yak is a very tame, often handsome, domestic animal, and a true bison in appearance. It is invaluable to these mountaineers from its strength and hardiness, accomplishing, at a slow pace, twenty miles a day, bearing either two bags of salt or rice, or four to six planks of pine-wood, slung in pairs along either flank.

11. "Their ears are generally pierced, and ornamented with a tuft of scarlet worsted; they have large and beautiful eyes, spreading horns, long silky black hair, and grand bushy tails. Black is their prevailing color. In winter the flocks graze below eight thousand feet, on account of the great quantity of snow above that height; in summer they find pasturage as high as seventeen thousand feet, consisting of grass and small tufted carices, which they browse with avidity. The yak is used as a beast of burden, and much of the wealth of the people consists in its rich milk and curd, eaten either fresh, or dried and powdered into a kind of meal. The hair is spun into ropes, and woven into a covering for their tents, which is quite pervious to wind or rain. The latter, however, is of little consequence in

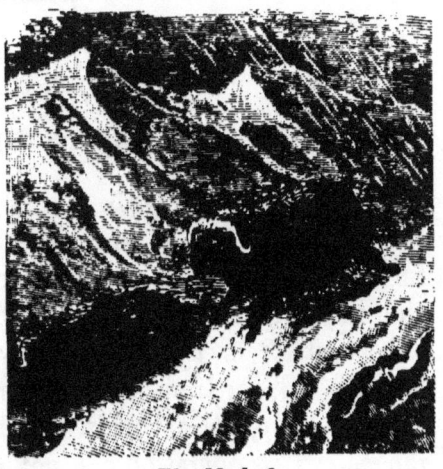

The Musk-Ox.

the dry climate of Thibet. The bushy tail forms the well-known fly-flapper of the plains of India."

12. "The musk-ox," says Figuier, "is much smaller than the common ox, and has somewhat the appearance of an enormous sheep. Its forehead is arched, its mouth small, its muzzle completely covered with hair; and its horns, which are very large, are closely united at the base, and bending downward over the sides of its head, suddenly turn backward and upward at the tips. Its long and abundant coat is of a dark brown color. It exhales a strong odor of musk, which even impregnates its flesh.

13. "This animal, which is a combination of the ox, sheep, and goat, inhabits North America below the polar circle, and lives in families of from ten to twenty individuals, among which there are seldom more than two or three males. Notwithstanding its apparent heaviness, the musk-ox climbs over the rocks almost as nimbly as a goat; and its speed across the rocky, rough, barren grounds, its principal habitat, for an animal so clumsy, is truly astonishing."

CHAPTER XXX.

THE RODEO OF THE LLANOS.

1. It is customary in all large cattle-ranches to assemble from time to time the cattle of certain districts for the purpose of selecting those which require branding and marking, and also to allow the neighboring *ranchers* to separate from the herds many stray animals belonging to them, which, from the open nature of the plains, it is impossible to keep within the boundaries of their own ranges. This operation can not be accomplished without

a great number of able and expert riders, who, on a given day, surround a large area of country, and drive toward

Lassoing Cattle.

one center all the cattle that may be found within the selected space. An extended circle or ring is thus formed, inclosing a great herd of wild animals; these are kept in check by the well-concerted evolutions of the *vaqueros*, until the appointed rendezvous is reached, where, after allowing the cattle to cool down, the different brands are selected; hence the name *rodeo*, from *rodear*, to surround.

2. The area selected for the *rodeo* embraced at least fifteen miles in circuit. The horsemen, in squads of six or eight, proceeded on the afternoon of the day before to their stations at various points, having instructions to start at early dawn for the appointed center. We of the staff made a simultaneous move from the house, driving before

us, without distinction, all the animals we encountered on the route. The cattle being so unexpectedly roused from their slumbers, naturally endeavored to fly from their pursuers. Soon, however, meeting those from opposite directions, they whirled in mad despair, vainly endeavoring to break through the extended line of horsemen, who were constantly galloping about the struggling mass with shouts and thrusts from their steel-pointed *garrochas*.

3. At the commencement it was a truly interesting sight to watch the many groups of cattle, deer, wild boars, dogs, foxes, and other wild quadrupeds, coming in from all directions as if impelled by one common instinct; but no sooner did that living ring commence closing upon them, than, scared by the confusion and uproar of the scene, their terror quickly grew to frenzy, and they ran from side to side, bellowing, grunting, howling, as they went. Solely intent upon the danger that menaced them, the mother forgot her offspring, and listened no more to their painful lamentations; and even the fierce bull forgetting for a moment that he is sovereign of those realms, lost his natural spirit of brave defiance, and rushed blindly off in the train of the frightened multitude.

4. As if to increase the grandeur of the spectacle, a crane, which had established itself on the borders of a creek hard by, also caught the alarm, and at our approach flew up in the air with a tremendous crashing of wing and bill, leaving her young to care for themselves, and with their discordant and piercing cries to swell the uproar of the scene. It is impossible to convey an adequate idea of this vast multitude of frightened cranes and herons of all sorts which fluttered overhead at that moment; so great was their number that they spread over an extent of several miles, and actually for a time cast a deep shadow over the landscape.

5. Not less than eight or ten thousand head of cattle were brought within the ring formed of more than a hundred horsemen, who, in preventing the escape of the animals, were compelled to expose themselves and their noble steeds to the vindictiveness of the bulls, which were constantly rushing upon the lines in their endeavors to regain the open prairies. Whenever this was attempted, a horseman galloped boldly upon the fugitive, and, by interposing himself between the open field and the bull, forced the latter back to the herd. Wonderfully adroit were the herdsmen in their avoidance of the repeated strokes aimed at them by the bulls, even when it appeared impossible to escape being caught between the animal's horns.

6. The *garrocha* played an important part in repelling these attacks. This instrument is made of the slender yet tough stem of the palm, by merely sharpening the top end to a point, or surmounting it with an iron head, around which a number of loose rings of the same metal are affixed; these, when shaken close to the animal's ear, frighten him off with the rattling-sound they produce. The shaft of the goad is fully ten feet long, and, although not thicker than a walking stick, can bear an immense amount of pressure without breaking. As a weapon of aggression, this slender palm-stem has become justly celebrated from the fact of having supplied the primitive bands of patriots who first dared to oppose the tyrannical rule of Spain with ready-made lances in the wilderness.

7. Some hours elapsed before the tremendous excitement and confusion of the wild *mêlée* described above had sufficiently subsided to render the forms of men and cattle visible through the clouds of dust and ashes raised by the trampling of so many animals. The grass, at this period parched by the sun and reduced to ashes in various places

by the usual conflagrations, mingled with the dust and rose in dense columns, which from afar might have been mistaken for the dreaded simoom. In the mean while the distracted mothers ran from side to side, lowing piteously for their missing young. Here and there fierce *duellos* among rival bulls took place. Butting their huge fronts together, and goring each other with their sharp-pointed horns, they fought with the courage and skill of accomplished gladiators, turning up the earth in wild fury, and filling the air with their deep, savage bellowing.

8. These sounds, with the yells and deafening shouts of the men galloping about the plain, waving their *ponchos* and rattling their *garrochas*, combined to give the scene more the appearance of a fiendish melodrama than a purely pastoral assemblage of men and cattle. The confusion having at length subsided, four of the ablest horsemen, penetrating the living mass, which, as they advanced, surged on either side like the waves of the sea, commenced the difficult task of separating the animals intended for the brand, and those belonging to our neighbors. This occasioned a series of evolutions which only men trained to such exercises could have accomplished successfully.

9. At all cattle-ranches it is usual to cut a notch or two in the animals' ears at the time they are branded, for the purpose of recognizing them more readily from a distance, a precaution which is particularly serviceable on occasions like that just described, it being impossible to read the brand when the creatures are crowded into a herd. Although most of the calves have not the notch, they belong by right to the owner of the mother, even if they are found with the herds of another party.

10. The separation of the cattle they accomplished in the most expeditious manner, by riding boldly at the animals

in question, hastening or checking their progress through the herd as the case demanded. Thus, by repeated evolutions of the sort, they finally brought the animals to the edge of the ring, where an opening was purposely left for their escape, and then the nearest horseman drove them in among a small band of tame cattle stationed a short distance from the *rodeo*. These violent, manœuvrings could not be accomplished, however, without endangering at every step the security of the entire herd.

11. Each time the drivers turned out an animal, the whole mass was thrown into the utmost confusion, and it required the most consummate skill on the part of the men to prevent the entire dispersion of the cattle. The fearlessness with which the drivers plunged into the labyrinth of savage, panting brutes, advancing close upon the wall of bristling horns, which barred their progress, and boldly driving the infuriated creatures before them like a pack of sheep, was truly worthy of admiration. The readiness with which they detected at a distance the mark on the animals' ears was also no less noticeable, singling out such at a glance, and immediately driving them away to their respective groups. When all the brands had been thus apportioned, each owner proceeded to drive away his own herd.

12. We found in these cases, as indeed in all similar ones, the assistance of *madrineros*, or trained oxen, of great service in driving a large body of cattle across the plains. But one of the most dangerous parts of the proceedings yet remained, that of forcing the cattle into the *corrals*. The entrance to the corral, shaped like a great funnel, was, like the rest of the fences, made of very strong posts, driven into the ground, and barred across at intervals with thick rafters of bamboo. Through this funnel, the cattle in small lots were driven at full speed, headed

by the *madrineros*, those treacherous guides trained to ensnare their kindred, while the horsemen barricaded the mouth of the funnel with the breasts of their horses.

13. Everything proceeded satisfactorily as far as the end of the funnel—the *madrineros*, with all the cunning of semi-civilized brutes, redoubling their pace at the moment of entering the great inclosure. Then, their wild brethren, perceiving their treachery, turned upon their captors, and a most fearful struggle ensued. The bulls, in spite of the deafening shouts of the men, and the formidable array of *garrochas* leveled at their heads, endeavored to force their way back to the open plain, and many of them actually succeeded in breaking through the barricade of horses.

14. That most of the men escaped unhurt, appeared little less than miraculous, as not only were they exposed at every moment to the vindictive attacks of the bulls, but it often happened that some of them were unhorsed, when they were in imminent danger of being trampled by the retreating foe. The superior skill and intrepidity of man, however, triumphed at length over mere brute resistance, and the whole herd was in a short time securely quartered in the corral.

Paez.

CHAPTER XXXI.

WOOL-BEARERS OF THE PASTURES.

1. It is an interesting fact that sheep were the first domestic animals to yield support to man. They were his original cattle, or *pecus*, and therefore constituted the main substance of his *pecuniary* condition. No other animals could have done so much for man. If we want other ani-

mals to clothe us, we must ask them to sacrifice their lives that we may have their skins. The sheep can keep its skin, and still cover us. Originally, sheep furnished milk as well as texture, and it was only when meat was demanded that they gave up their lives; and just in proportion to the care man has bestowed upon these timid and defenseless animals has been the reward they have yielded him.

2. The property and wealth of the ancient patriarchs

The Merino Sheep.

consisted in sheep. From them has descended to us in an almost unbroken line the Spanish merino. The so-called native sheep of America, like our native cattle, have no definite origin; but the lineage of the merino is ancient and clean; and this is what gives to the breed its clearly-marked and distinguishing characteristics. The impression of several thousand years is stamped upon it. Once seen, it will be known again as readily as a Chinaman is recognized. The merino is, *par excellence*, the sheep of fine wool. Its fleece is short, and grows in a thick mat, oily, and therefore dirty in appearance, covering the cheeks, and lying up in ridges and ruffles about the neck.

3. The sheep of coarse-wool fleeces are animals of larger frame. Their definite origin can scarcely be traced. The wild sheep, under the care and skill of human intelligence, is susceptible of improvement in almost any desired direction. The coat of the sheep in its wild state is a mixture of short hair and wool. With care exercised in the selection of the offspring, and assistance in procuring its food, this coat has grown less hair and more wool; then, with favorable conditions of climate and pasture, size of frame, qualities of flesh, and length of wool have been obtained. In this way has come the Southdown of England, the famous mutton-sheep, easily distinguished by its round body, medium wool, and dark-brown head and legs. The lambs of the Southdown, large and plump, join with green peas to give to market-stalls the flavor of spring.

4. The Leicester and Cotswold breeds are highly esteemed in England where they originated, and in America where they have been introduced. They carry the largest frames and the longest wool. For mutton they are good; but their fleeces attain to a great weight. No animals among the domestic tribes more strikingly show the effects of liberal care than do these large, white, woolly, clean-faced sheep. Upon the Highlands of Scotland, or among the rocks where wild sheep and goats flourish, they would die. Fat pastures, level footing, shelter from rough weather, and high feeding, are absolutely necessary to their existence. They are the pampered aristocracy of their race, and there is little poetry about them, except

when a small group of them give picturesque life to a distant lawn.

5. The sheep of ancient pastoral life is of a different

Sheep-washing in Australia.

sort. It was smaller, more nimble of foot, and hardy of constitution. Its large, hollow horns, long since depending upon the protection of the pastor, or shepherd, seemed at a loss what to do with themselves; so they have grown downward and curled about like an Alpine horn. These animals love the rocky steeps, and nibble the sweet scattered tufts of the mountain-sides. The shepherd boy, or girl, with crook or staff and faithful dogs, are their constant attendants. From these groups have originated those delicious pastoral scenes from which the poets have gathered the choice substance of their idyls and madrigals. Our pampered and fence-inclosed flocks can give little idea of those charming sketches of pastoral life.

6. Of the domestic sheep Buffon says: "This species

appears to be preserved only by the assistance and care of man; it seems unable to subsist by itself. The reclaimed sheep is absolutely without resource and without defense. The ram is but weakly armed; its courage is only petulance. The females are still more timid than the males. It is fear that causes them to assemble in flocks. The slightest noise makes them throw themselves down headlong or crowd one against the other; and this fear is accompanied with the greatest stupidity, for they know not how to avoid danger. They appear not even to see the inconveniences of their situation; they remain obstinately where they are exposed to rain or snow. In order to oblige them to change their situation and take a certain road, a leader is necessary, whose movements they follow at every step. This leader would himself remain motionless with the rest of the flock if he were not driven by the shepherd or excited by the sheep-dog, which knows well how to defend, direct, separate, reassemble them, and communicate to them all necessary movements.

7. "They are of all animals the most devoid of resources. Goats, which resemble them in so many other respects, have much more sense. They know how to guide themselves; they avoid danger and easily familiarize themselves with new objects, while the sheep neither retreats nor advances, and allows its lamb to be taken away without anger or resistance or even signifying its grief by a cry differing from its usual bleat. Nevertheless, this creature, so helpless and apathetic, is to mankind the most valuable of all animals, and of the most immediate and extensive use. Alone it suffices for his most pressing wants, furnishing both food and clothing, besides the various uses of fat, milk, skin, entrails, bones, and manure. Nature seems to have bestowed nothing upon the sheep that does not serve for the advantage of the human race."

8. The structure of wool is different from that of hair, and fits it perfectly for twisting into yarn and for rolling into felting. Wool was wrought into garments at a very early period. Many passages in the Bible history allude to woolen garments. At the time of the Macedonian conquest the natives of India wore shawls of great beauty. The Greeks learned many processes of woolen manufacture from the Egyptians; and the Romans, as well as the people of Spain, obtained instruction in this art from the Greeks. In these days the manufacture of goods from the fleeces of sheep is an immense industry. No less than thirty-five processes are passed through to transmute the wool into cloth. Among these are sorting the wool, scouring, washing, drying, dyeing, carding, spinning, reeling, weaving, shearing, and fulling.

9. The simplicity and charm of ancient times are still retained among the shepherds of the half-civilized tribes

Tartars and their Flocks.

of Asia. The Tartars and Siberians and the natives of Thibet still follow the nomadic life of mountain-shepherds. The pastures of different localities and varying altitudes in the mountains and table-lands produce their abundance at different times of the year; hence the flocks and their faithful guardians must move. These people in their rude way manufacture the wool of their flocks into blankets and articles of personal apparel.

10. The Asiatic argali, a large, powerful sheep about three feet high and weighing two hundred pounds, is the original wild sheep of the mountains of Asia, and the source of a valuable domestic breed. Its heavy and awkward horns would seem to be a burden rather than a means of defense. The kebsch is an African species, and is remarkable for its long mane, which feature has led some writers to class it as a goat. Our Rocky Mountain sheep is an argali, and is called a big-horn from the great size of these ornaments of the head. It inhabits the northern regions of the Rocky Mountains and the Yellowstone.

CHAPTER XXXII.

MOUNTAIN MILK-GIVERS.

1. THE goat is closely related to the sheep, from which it differs in features that are familiar. The horns worn by both sexes always turn or curve backward; the covering is more of hair than of wool; the chin is bearded, and the tail, like that of the deer, is short. "The goat has more intelligence than the sheep, and soon becomes familiar and attached; it is light, active, and less timid than the sheep. It is capricious, and loves to wander, to climb steep mountains, sleeping frequently on the point of a rock or on the edge of a precipice. It is robust, and will feed on almost any plant." Its milk is said to be more

digestible than that of cows, and in many mountain-regions it is valued for its milk products, cheese and butter. The skins of the goat and kid are valued in the manufacture of fine shoes and gloves.

2. The Rocky Mountain goat resembles the merino sheep in figure and size. Its horns are small, conical, smooth, nearly erect, and jet-black. Its outer hair is long, straight, white, and soft, and hangs down all over the body. It inhabits the highest and most inaccessible parts of the Rocky Mountains, and is very difficult to procure. The cashmere goat, whose home is in Thibet, has long, straight, silky hair, large pendent ears, and slender legs. Its fleece has become famous by the rare texture of the fabrics into which it enters. The cashmere shawls have great value, and the kingdom of Cashmere, in India, has built up an extensive industry in the manufacture of these articles. It operates sixteen thousand looms, and turns out thirty thousand shawls annually. It requires a year to make a single shawl of a rich pattern.

The Rocky Mountain Goat.

3. The angora goat, which takes its name from the city of Angora, in Asia Minor, nearly resembles the cashmere species. Its hair is not straight, but hangs in long, flowing tresses of spiral ringlets. Its fleece is used in the manufacture of beautiful light fabrics called zephyr-cloths.

The angora has been successfully raised in France, and in the Southern States of this country. It is more tractable and amiable in disposition than our common goat.

4. The ibex inhabits the mountainous parts of Europe, and combines the general character of the goat with the fleetness of the antelope. Colonel Markham says of it: "All readers of natural history are familiar with the wonderful climbing and leaping powers of the ibex; and although they can not (as has been described in print) make a spring and hang by the horns until they gain a footing, yet in reality, for such heavy animals, they get over the most inaccessible-looking places in an almost miraculous manner. Nothing seems to stop them, nor to impede their progress in the least.

The Common Ibex.

5. "To see a flock, after being fired at, take a distant line across country, which they often do, over all sorts of seemingly impassable ground, now along the naked surface of an almost perpendicular rock, then across a formidable land-slip, or an inclined plane of loose stones or sand, which the slightest touch sets in motion, both above and below, diving into chasms to which there seems no possible outlet, but instantly reappearing on the opposite side, never deviating in the slightest from their course, and at

the same time getting over the ground at the rate of something like fifteen miles an hour, is a sight not easily to be forgotten.

6. "The goat possesses great natural affection for its young, and uses both courage and artifice in their defense. The fox, which is the particular enemy of the whole of the sheep kind, does not fail to attempt to seize the young of the goat. When the mother discovers the fox approaching, while the insidious foe is yet at a distance, she conceals her offspring in some thicket, and interposes herself between it and the wily marauder. The kid, when conveyed to this retreat, invariably lies close and still, as if, according to the fable, she had received the verbal instructions of the dam. But the fox generally discovers the retreat of the kid, and a contest ensues between the rapacious and the affectionate animal. The manner of these contests is illustrated by the following anecdote, which furnishes an affecting instance at once of the courage and of the love of its offspring possessed by the goat:

7. "A person having missed one of his goats when his flock was taken home at night, and being afraid the wanderer would get among the young trees of his nursery, two boys, wrapped in their plaids, were ordered to watch all night. The morning had faintly dawned, when they sprang up the hill in search of her. They could but just discern her on a pointed rock afar off; and, hastening to the spot, perceived her standing with a newly-dropped kid which she was defending against a fox. The enemy turned round and round to lay hold of his prey, but the goat presented her horns in every direction.

8. "The youngest boy was dispatched to get assistance to attack the fox, and the eldest, hallooing and throwing up stones, sought to intimidate him as he climbed to rescue his charge. The fox seemed well aware that the

child could not execute his threats; he looked at him one instant, and then renewed the assault, till, quite impatient, he made a sudden effort to seize the kid. The whole three disappeared, and were found at the bottom of the precipice. The goat's horns were darted into the back of the fox; the kid lay stretched beside her. It is supposed the fox had fixed his teeth in the kid, for its neck was lacerated; but, when the faithful mother inflicted a death-wound upon her mortal enemy, he probably staggered, and brought his victim with him over the rock."

9. "A gentleman who had taken an active share in the rebellion of 1715, after the battle of Preston escaped to the West Highlands, to the residence of a female relative who afforded him an asylum. As it was soon judged unsafe for him to remain in the house of his friend, he was conducted to a cavern in a sequestered situation, and furnished with a supply of food. The approach to this lonely abode consisted of a small aperture, through which he crept and dragged his provisions along with him. A little way from the mouth the roof became elevated, but, on advancing, an obstacle obstructed his progress; unwilling to strike at a venture with his dirk, he stooped down and discovered a goat and her kid lying on the ground.

10. "He soon perceived that the animal was in great pain, and, feeling her body and limbs, ascertained that one of her legs was fractured. He bound it up with his garter, and offered her some of his bread; but she refused to eat, and stretched out her tongue, as if intimating that her mouth was parched with thirst. He gave her water, which she drank greedily, and then she ate the bread. At midnight he ventured from the cave, pulled a quantity of grass and the tender branches of trees, and carried them to the poor sufferer, who received them with demonstrations of gratitude. The only thing which this fugi-

tive had to arrest his attention in his drear abode was administering comfort to the goat; and he was indeed thankful to have any living creature beside him.

11. "The goat quickly recovered, and became tenderly attached to him. It happened that the servant who was intrusted with the secret of his retreat fell sick, when it became necessary to send another with provisions. The goat, on this occasion, happening to be lying near the mouth of the cavern, opposed his entrance with all her might, butting him furiously; the fugitive, hearing a disturbance, went forward, and, receiving the watchword from his new attendant, interposed, and the faithful goat permitted him to pass. So resolute was the animal on this occasion that the gentleman was convinced she would die in his defense."

CHAPTER XXXIII.

AGILE DWELLERS OF MOUNTAIN AND PLAIN.

"I'll chase the antelope over the plain,
The tiger's cub I will bind with a chain,
And the wild gazelle with its silvery feet
I will give thee for a playmate sweet."

1. THE antelope is one of those creatures that remind us of the essential unity of different animal tribes. It bears strong resemblances to the ox, the goat, and the deer. Like the ox and the goat, it has hollow, and, in most cases, permanent horns. Its ability to spring and climb is similar to though far surpassing that of the goat; while in size, general outline of form, and habits of life, it resembles the deer. Its horns are more like those of the goat, curving backward, and in some varieties again

turning in like the frame of a lyre. Most of the antelopes are remarkable for their graceful and slender make, the structure of their limbs being beautifully adapted for rapid flight. Their eyes are large and lustrous, and their sight and scent remarkably keen.

2. The American antelope, or prong-buck, of the Rocky Mountain region is much smaller than the common deer. It is said to possess glands from which a pungent odor is emitted like that of the goat. The eye of our antelope is much larger than that of the deer, the ox, or the horse; is intensely black, and is softened with a mild and gentle expression. This animal is one of the swiftest-footed of all quadrupeds, and its speed is like the flight of a bird. Its horizontal leaps are of astonishing length, though it refuses to vault over even a moderately high fence. Its horns, which divide into two prongs near the tip, are hollow; but there is good authority to believe that, like the antlers of the deer, they fall off and are renewed.

3. "The antelopes of America are lean. Being fleet and quick-sighted, they are generally the victims of their curiosity, for when they first see the hunter they run with great velocity. If he lies down on the ground and lifts up his arm, his hat, or his foot, the antelope returns on a light trot to look at the object, and sometimes comes and goes two or three times, till it gets within reach of the rifle. Sometimes, too, they leave their own herd to go and look at the wolves, who crouch down, and, if the antelope be frightened at first, they repeat the same manœuvre, and sometimes relieve each other, till they get it completely separated from the rest of the herd, when they seize it; but generally the wolves seize the antelopes while they are crossing the rivers, for though swift of foot they are bad swimmers."

4. The chamois of the Alpine mountains, though like the goat in appearance, is a true antelope. A short, sudden turn backward of the tips of its horns distinguishes it from all other antelopes. Attached to its hind-feet are false hoofs, which render efficient aid to this animal when it descends precipitous rocks. With these hoofs it hitches and catches on every irregularity of rock or shrub in its downward slide. It does not hesitate to leap down an almost perpendicular precipice of twenty or thirty feet.

The Chamois.

5. "They are keen of scent, shy, and vigilant. When the herd either feeds or reposes, one of the number is posted on some rock to leeward of them to give warning of approaching danger, and his instant shrill whistle is repeated by all, the younger ones escaping to windward, while some skip in great agitation from rock to rock to reconnoitre till they are reassured or move off, always, if possible, in ascent toward the most inaccessible cliffs. If the hunter pursues them until one is driven to some point from which there is no retreat, it is said that it will pitch itself down upon its foe and dash him into the abyss below."

6. The gazelles, with incurved, lyre-shaped horns, are described as "easily recognizable by their large, round black horns, and equally remarkable for the lightness of their form and the elegance of their proportions. They

inhabit the vast continent of Africa, through which they roam in prodigious herds that sometimes appear innumerable, and where they constitute the ordinary prey of the lion and the panther. Nevertheless, when attacked they are not without some means of defense. Under such circumstances, if there is time for such a manœuvre, arranging themselves in a circular phalanx they present their formidable horns, disposed as thickly as the bayonets of a regiment of soldiers, and when thus disposed their array is not easily broken."

7. "As the traveler advances from the Cape toward the Sahara, he constantly falls in with new antelopes, and many unknown to the naturalist, no doubt, will still roam in the undiscovered interior of the continent. With the exception of the ox or cow-like species, such as the eland, whose clumsier proportions and heavier gait remind one of our domestic cattle, the antelopes generally resemble the deer tribe by their elegant forms, their restless and timid disposition, and their proverbial swiftness. Their horns, whatever shape they assume, are round and annulated, in some species straight, in others curved and spiral. In some the females have no horns; in others they are common to both sexes. They all possess a most delicate sense of smell, and their eyes are proverbially bright and beaming. The largest of all the antelope tribe is the bubale, or wild ox of the Arabs.

8. "Few of the numerous African antelopes are more entitled to our notice than the graceful spring-bok, which has earned its name from the surprising and almost perpendicular leaps it makes when startled. It bounds to the height of ten or twelve feet with the elasticity of an India-rubber ball, clearing at each leap from twelve to fifteen feet of ground without apparently the slightest exertion. In performing this astonishing leap, it appears for an in-

stant as if suspended in the air, when down come all four feet again together, and, striking the plain, away it soars as if about to take flight."

The Bubale.

9. "I have," says Mr. Drummond, "personally ridden down the eland on several occasions, though, as they are the slowest antelope in Africa, it is no great feat to do so. Sometimes a young cow in low condition will give one a real gallop, there being much the same difference between it and a corpulent old bull as between a wild young Highland two-year-old able with ease to clear a five-barred gate and a stall-fed ox fit for Smithfield."

10. The giraffe, or camelopard, has its home in South-

ern Africa. It is an animal of striking appearance and many resemblances. It is a ruminant with permanent horns in both sexes. A careful study of its features will discover in the giraffe a likeness to the camel, the ox, the deer, the antelope, the goat, and the ostrich. It is the tallest four-footed animal in existence, measuring in some cases from eighteen to twenty feet from the top of its head to the ground. "Its feet, which are like those of the goat, endow it with the dexterity of that animal. It bounds over wide ravines with incredible power. Horses can not in such situations compete with it.

The Giraffe and its Neighbors.

11. "The giraffe is fond of a wooded country. The leaves of trees are its principal food. Green herbs are

also very agreeable to this animal; but its structure does not admit of its feeding on them in the same manner as our other domestic animals, such as the ox and the horse. It is obliged to straddle widely. Its two fore-feet are gradually stretched apart from each other, and its neck being then bent in a semicircular form, the animal is thus enabled to collect the grass; but on the instant that any noise interrupts its repast, it raises itself with rapidity and takes to immediate flight. The giraffe eats with great delicacy and takes its food leaf by leaf, collecting them from the trees by means of its long tongue. It rejects the thorns, and in this respect differs from the camel."

12. "The giraffe during flight," says Anderssen, "does not move the limbs of either side alternately, but swings forward the two legs of the same side at the same instant, so that it is one of the most curious sights imaginable to see a troop of these animals at full speed, balancing themselves to and fro in a manner not easily described, and whisking their tails tufted at the end, while their long and tapering necks, swaying backward and forward, follow the motion of their bodies." And Dr. Livingstone says: "Such is the strength of these colossal quadrupeds that they are not to be approached without danger, and we are told that old sportsmen are careful not to go too close to a giraffe's tail, for this animal can swing his hindfoot round in a way which would leave little to choose between a kick with it and a blow from the arm of a windmill."

13. After man, the giraffe's chief enemy is the lion, who often waits for it in the thick brakes on the margin of the rivers or pools, and darts upon it with a murderous spring while it is slaking its thirst. Anderssen once saw five lions, two of whom were in the act of pulling down a splendid giraffe, while the other three were watching close

at hand the deadly strife ; and Captain Harris relates that, while he was encamped on the banks of a small stream, a camelopard was killed by a lion while in the act of drinking at no great distance from the wagons. It was a noisy affair ; but an inspection of the scene on which it occurred proved that the giant strength of the victim had been paralyzed in an instant.

14. One of the most singular of all the antelope species

The Gnu.

is the gnu, or, as it is popularly called, the "horned horse." At first sight it has the appearance of being made up of portions of several other quadrupeds. It is about the size of a half-grown colt, and it has the body and croup of a horse. It is covered with short, brown hair, and it has a white tail, flowing like that of a horse. It has, moreover, a mane upon the center of its neck. At a distance it is said to resemble the lion.

15. But, in spite of its appearance, the gnu is a true ruminant, and a near kin to the other antelopes, with whom it associates. It has low, bent horns, something like those of the Cape buffalo, and it is furnished with cloven feet, which exhibit all the lightness of those of a stag. The flesh resembles venison, and is highly esteemed by both hunters and natives.

16. Captain Harris says: "While crossing the wide plains of the Vaal River we had an opportunity of remarking the very similar appearance of the lion and the gnu, and in twice witnessing the animated but abortive pursuit of a herd of gnus by an enormous lion, rendered furious by the qualms of hunger, and still more desperately frantic by the disappointment entailed by the slippery heels of his intended victims, who, on both occasions, left their grim pursuer far behind, puffing and blowing, to grumble over the loss of the morning repast which he had vainly promised himself."

CHAPTER XXXIV.

ANTLERED TENANTS OF THE WOODS.

"I know where the timid fawn abides
In the depths of the shaded dell,
Where the leaves are broad and the thicket hides,
With its many stems and its tangled sides,
From the eye of the hunter well."

1. THE parent of this "timid fawn," so artfully hidden, and whose secret place the Indian knows so well, is

the American or Virginian deer. It belongs to that class of ruminating animals the males of which carry large branching, solid horns, that fall off and are renewed every year. The deer-hunt in the wilder regions of North America is an exciting sport, and often trying to the nerves of the young and inexperienced sportsman. A writer in "Scribner's Monthly" gives a graphic sketch of such an occasion, from which the following descriptive selections are made:

2. " The deer of the region is the *Cervus Virginianus*, or common deer of America, which is distributed over

The Red Deer with Branching Antlers.

such a large area of our continent. Of the deer killed by our party, there were no less than three that weighed over two hundred and twenty-five pounds. It is the most beautiful of the *Cervidæ*, and in its graceful carriage, its exquisite agility, and the delicacy and symmetry of its form, no other animal approaches it. The eye of the deer is large, and has the softest and most tender expression.

3. "The fawns, betraying by their spots a former characteristic of their species, are timid, pretty little things. They do not seem to have the instinct which leads the adult animal to the water when pursued, and consequently, when the dog gets on the scent of a fawn, he will hunt it bootlessly for hours, to the great annoyance of his master. A young fawn, just born, knows no fear of man. If picked up, fondled for a few minutes, and carried a little distance, it will, when put down, follow one just as it would its mother.

4. "A tremendous uproar awoke me at the moment when, for the hundredth time, my rifle had exasperated me. It was Mr. B—— shouting: 'Breakfast! breakfast! Turn out for breakfast! The captain's up and waiting!' It was half-past four, and everybody woke up at the summons, as was, indeed, unavoidable. Down-stairs there was a prodigious sizzling and sputtering going on, and the light through the floor betrayed Mrs. Brumfield and her frying-pans and coffee-pot, all in full blast. We were all down-stairs in a few minutes and outside making a rudimentary toilet with ice-water and a bar of soap. Breakfast was ready—plenty of rashers of bacon, fried and boiled potatoes, fried onions, bread and butter, and coffee, hot and strong.

5. "These were speedily disposed of. Coats were buttoned up, rubber blankets and ammunition-belts slung over shoulders, cartridge magazines filled, hatchets stuck into belts, rifles shouldered, and out we sallied into the darkness, through which the faintest glimmer of gray was just showing in the east. After a couple of hundred

yards of climb, crawl, and tumble through one of the swamps, my companion took his place under the shelter of the cedars, and indicated mine at a little distance up the river. The wind howled down through the trees, and clouds of yellow and russet leaves came sailing into the river, and hurried away upon the surface. I was undeniably, miserably cold.

6. "But hark! I seized my rifle. Yes, there it was, sure enough, the bay of the dog in the distance! I forgot

Bucks fighting.

to be cold. Nearer it came, and nearer and nearer, and each moment I thought would bring the deer crashing through the thickets into the river. Nearer and nearer came the dogs, until their deep bays resounded and echoed through the forest as if they were in a great hall. But no deer appeared, and the dogs held their course, on, down, parallel with the river. 'Better luck next time,' I said to myself, somewhat disconsolately; but I was disappointed. Presently the sharp, ringing crack of a rifle rang out and reverberated across the forest; another and another followed, and, as I began to get cold again, I tried to console myself by meditating on the luck of other people.

7. "At camp, the doctor was the center of an animated circle. He was most unreasonably composed, as I thought, and told us, with his German equanimity, how Jack and Pedro had run in a large buck, which immediately swam down the middle of the river. He fired from his place on the side of a bluff, and missed. At the second shot he succeeded in hitting the deer in the neck. As if this were not sufficient, there presently appeared a very pretty fawn, whose young hopes were promptly blighted. During the afternoon, Curtis brought both deer up to camp and dressed them. The buck was finely antlered, and was estimated to weigh two hundred pounds.

8. "Six days passed, and a dozen deer were hanging in the barn, and I was quite guiltless of the death of any of them. The next day, five deer were killed, without any participation upon my part, and in the evening some of us, with lanterns, went down to the river to secure one that had lodged somewhere in the drift-wood. We found it by the light of the birch-bark. As we made our way along the bank, our backwoodsman would pick out here and there a large white birch, and apply a match to the curling ringlets of bark at the foot of the trunk. In a moment the whole stem of the tree was in a roaring blaze that lit up the river-bank all round about, and made the great cedars look like gigantic skeletons.

9. "Next morning I was at my place, subdued and hopeful. I heard a shot fired on the river below me; I

heard the baying of the dogs, and listened to it as it died away in the direction of some other runway. But I watched steadily. And as I watched I saw the brush about some cedar-roots open, and out there sprang into the shallow water a noble buck. He was a stalwart, thickset fellow, his legs were short and compact, his fur was dark in its winter hue, and his antlers glistened above his head. He bore himself proudly, as he stood in the water and turned to listen for the bay of the dogs he had outrun.

10. "I hesitated a moment, doubtful if I should let him go into the stream and swim down, or shoot him as he stood. I chose the latter, aimed quietly and confidently, and fired. He pitched forward; the current seized him, and he floated down with it past me, dead. In eight minutes by my watch Mr. M——'s "Jack" came to the bank, at the spot where the buck had come in, and howled grievously over the lost scent. He was worn out and battered, and he came to me gladly when I called him.

11. "I had brought some luncheon down with me in the morning, and I must confess that I was weak enough to give Jack every bit of it. That afternoon, when I reached camp, I found that I was the last to come in, and that my buck had already been seen, and his size noted. I was received with acclamations, and a proposition to gird me, as a measure of affected precaution, with the hoops of a flour-barrel, was made and partly carried into execution. There were sung, moreover, sundry snatches of the foresters' chorus from 'As You Like It':

'What shall he have that killed the deer?'"

12. The elk, or moose, the largest of the deer tribe, is distinguished by its great size, its awkward shape, and its broad, palmated horns. A writer in the magazine above

quoted says: "A full-grown moose sheds his horns in the month of January, and they are not restored again until the end of August. By this time the velvet has been worn off, and the horns are a rich fawn-color, shaded or marked with dark brown, and polished by having been rubbed on the stems of the poplar and larch. The fights which now occur between the old males are terrific.

The Moose.

Greek has met Greek, and the combat is often prolonged until their horns become inextricably interlaced, and both animals die a miserable death.

13. "Early in May, the cow-moose brings forth two, sometimes three calves, of a dark fawn-color, and slightly dappled. It has been affirmed that the cow-moose retires to some sequestered spot, in order to protect her young from the attacks of bears, and also of the bull-moose; but I am of opinion that the latter is not, at any time, very distant from the cow and her calves. On one occasion, in the early summer, I saw an old cow-moose with two calves come out from an island in a lake and disport in the water. Presently a bull-moose came out of the forest, at a little distance from them, and began to eat the roots of the yellow pond-lily, which he procured by diving for them and bringing them to the surface of the water in his teeth. While he was still feeding the cow and her calves retired."

CHAPTER XXXV.

THE LAPLANDER'S TREASURE.

1. THE American caribou answers to the reindeer of the extreme north of Europe. It roams over a vast range of territory, being found as far south as Maine, in Newfoundland, and on the bleak barrens of Labrador. Like the reindeer, both sexes of the caribou wear large, branching antlers; and they are compact in form and possessed of great speed. The color of the caribou is dark fawn, or light gray; that of the Lapland reindeer is brown, growing white as winter approaches. The caribou, or reindeer of America, is the game of the Indian or the sportsman, and is never domesticated. The Lapp reindeer is found wild in large numbers, but is chiefly noted as the domestic animal of many uses to the inhabitants of a barren, winter land; and this is a description of it and its home, given by Mr. Bowden:

2. "The reindeer furnishes its master, the wandering Lapp, or native of Norwegian Lapland, with food; warm fur coats are made from its skin, as well as excellent leather; spoons, forks, and other articles are made from its horns; while the only household gods that the poor Lapp possesses are made from the bones, sinews, or muscles of the same serviceable creature. The reindeer also draws its master's sledge, and transports his worldly goods from one place to another. The nerves and sinews of the animal are dried; then they are softened by being steeped for some days in water, when they are worked up and made into an article resembling flax. A substance as fine as cotton, and much stronger, is manufactured from this flax. The weaving apparatus looks like a large white comb, and is made of the broad, frontal horns of the rein-

deer. The hide is tanned, and makes strong, durable harness, boots, and other articles.

Lapps and Reindeer.

3. "The reindeer harness is of leather, manufactured from the hide of the animal. It is very strong, and is ornamented with scarlet cloth; for the Lapp has a mania for bright colors. The scarlet housings are adorned with the hair of the deer, dyed black for the purpose, and embroidered artistically; the scarlet and black colors form an agreeable contrast. In speaking of the harness we allude to the collar which goes around the reindeer's neck, as well as the reins which are fastened to it. The initials of the owner's name are worked on this scarlet collar with black thread. The reindeer is fastened to the sledge by a single strap, so that it is harnessed in a moment, and is then ready to start off on its journey. The traveling-

sledge is made of birch-wood; it is pointed at the end, runs on a kind of wide keel, and resembles a coffin in shape. It travels with incredible swiftness over the snow.

4. "When a colony of Lapps is moving from place to place, their numerous sledges have a rather pretty effect. This is especially the case when a number of sledges, drawn by reindeer, are passing over a broad sheet of frozen water. The sledges, the Lapps with their wives and children, and the numbers of the dogs, running at the top of their speed, render the sight a most novel and interesting one. The tame reindeer is by no means of an amiable disposition. It is by nature vicious, and, when drawing the sledge, the Lapp has but little control over it; it often becomes restive, stands suddenly still, and kicks out behind. Then it will occasionally stop when running at full speed, turn round, and coolly attack its driver with its horns.

5. "In this predicament the Lapp turns the sledge completely over, and gets underneath; the reindeer then pokes away at the sledge with its horns, but injures itself more than its master. When the vicious brute has expended its wrath in this manner, and ceases its attack on the sledge, the Lapp quietly emerges, sets the sledge on its keel again, seizes the reins once more, and continues his journey as if nothing unusual had happened.

6. "Like the wild reindeer, the tame species has many enemies, and numbers fall victims to the bear, the wolf, and the glutton. The tame reindeer is neither so bold nor so powerful an animal as the wild, and, when attacked by beasts of prey, it makes but little resistance. The tame reindeer feeds principally upon various kinds of lichens, and is driven to the fjelds in summer to search for them. In winter it finds the same kind of food under

the snow, when its frontal horns are very useful in scraping away the snow from the places where the lichens grow.

7. " When out grazing on the fjelds, the reindeer are prevented from wandering too far by men who are regularly employed to watch them, and who are assisted in their labors by dogs. Some Lapps have as many as forty dogs to keep the reindeer together, and to drive them home to be milked. These animals are as sagacious as English sheep-dogs, and can distinguish their respective charges by some instinctive recognition of their faces. The Lapp is neither kind nor gentle to his dogs, but keeps them in a state of semi-starvation—they have to depend for their food on the bones of the reindeer that are thrown to them, or to the licking out of the pots as they lie round the Lapp's tent. A grim joke is extant in Norway, to the effect that the Lapp is too lazy to clean his pots and pans, so he keeps his dogs hungry to do it for him.

Reindeer and Glutton.

8. "A reindeer-cheese is a particularly unpleasant-looking article of food. It is flat and round, like a huge muffin. Its flavor is very little better than its look. It is said that the oil extracted from a reindeer-cheese by holding it before the fire is, if applied to the affected part, a sure remedy for the cure of frost-bite. When residing among them, the food is the most trying part of the affair, for one soon tires of reindeer-venison. Breakfast among this primitive people consists of reindeer-milk, to which all help themselves out of the same pot, and generally with the same spoon. The dinner consists of reindeer venison and soup; at the supper, reindeer-cheese is served out.

9. "When the meal is ready, the master of the household takes his place near the huge copper pan in which the reindeer venison and soup are cooked; the wife, children, and servants, range themselves in a row, waiting to begin. The head of the family then gravely sticks his fork into a piece of venison, drags it out, and begins to eat it. The others do the same, and the only respect paid to the master is this: when a servant hooks out a piece of venison that is particularly fat and inviting, he puts it into the pot again, giving his master a grin as he does so, as much as to say, 'That belongs to you by right, O master!' When this is done, the master gives a grunt of satisfaction, and complacently sticks his fork into the reserved morsel of venison."

CHAPTER XXXVI.

THE SHIP OF THE DESERT.

1. THE camel is a four-footed, ruminating animal so peculiarly adapted to traverse great seas of sand that it is called in the figurative language of Eastern nations the "ship of the desert." It is found in Asia and Africa, where it is used for transportation over the broad and barren plains destitute of both food and water. There are

The Arabian Camel.

two species, the Bactrian camel of Asia, which has two humps on its back, and the Arabian camel, which has but one hump. The two-humped animal walks with more ease over moist ground, and is larger and stronger than the other. The Arabian camel is sober and possessed of great powers of endurance. The lightest and swiftest of this sort are called dromedaries, and are used chiefly to carry passengers. The flesh and milk of this animal are used for food, and their hair is made into clothing, shawls, and carpets.

2. The camel has on each foot two toes, which are united and covered underneath by a sole or tough pad, which adapts it for pressing upon the sand, but would be useless on rocky or slippery ground. "From time immemorial," says Figuier, "the camel has been the only means of bearing commodities across the desert. By means of this patient and strong animal, merchandise finds its way from the remote countries of Asia as far as the eastern confines of Europe. The rich products of Arabia, ages past, were brought to Phœnicia on the backs of camels; and in our time, in the same way, merchandise is borne to Alexandria, whence it is distributed over the European Continent.

The Camel's Foot.

3. "The better to fit the camel for its arduous life, the Arab trains it to do without sleep, and to suffer all the extremes of hunger, thirst, and heat. A few days after its birth its legs are bent under its stomach, and it is compelled to remain crouched upon the ground laden with a suitable weight, which is gradually increased with its age. As it arrives at maturity its food is restricted and given at longer intervals; it is also practiced in running and enduring severe exercise.

4. "A camel laden with five or six hundred pounds' weight will travel eight or ten leagues a day under a burning sun with no other food than a few handfuls of grain, a small number of dates, or a little pellet of maize-paste. It will go ten days without drinking; but when it approaches a pool it scents it at a great distance, redoubles its pace, eagerly pushes for the coveted necessary of life, and drinks for the past, the present, and, alas! too often for a long future."

5. The faculty which the camel possesses of dispensing with water for a long time is due to the fact that it carries internally a reservoir of water, which it uses in case of necessity. The digestive organs, like that of other ruminants, is composed of four different stomachs. There is also a bag which is divided into cubical receptacles or reservoirs for water. The ability to endure a long time without food is explained by the hump on the camel's back. This hump incloses a large amount of fat, which is absorbed by the hungry system and operates as nourishment. After a long and weary journey the hump collapses and the animal grows thin.

The Camel's Head.

6. From the description of George William Curtis we learn that "a camel excites no sentiment or affection in the Western,

nor did I observe any indication of the Arab's love for the animal. He is singularly adapted to his business of walking over the desert, but is awkward and cross, and destitute of any agreeable trait. His motion is ludicrously stiff and slow. He advances as if his advent were the coming of grace and beauty, and the carriage of his neck and head is comically conceited beyond words. My camel never suggested a pleasurable emotion to me but once, and that was on the first morning, when, as we moved from camp, he lifted his head toward the desert and sniffed as if he tasted home and his natural freedom in the polluted air.

7. "The camels seem to be only half tamed; and sometimes, seduced by the fascination of the desert's breath, they break from the caravan and dash away in a wild, grotesque trot, straight into the grim silence of the wilderness, bearing the luckless Howadji upon a voyage too vague, and pursued by the yells and moans of the Bedoueen. They are guided by a halter slipped behind their ears and over the nose, and they swing their flexible necks like ostriches.

8. "In the first desert days I sometimes thought to alter the direction of my beast by pulling the halter; but I gathered in its whole length, hand over hand, and only drew the long neck quite round, so that the great stupid head was almost between my knees, and the hateful eyes stared mockingly at my own. I learned afterward to guide the animal by touching the side of the neck with a stick.

9. "The pasha's was a smaller beast than mine, and looked and acted like a cassowary. The Arabs called him El Shiraz, and the commander's was dubbed Pomegranate by the same relentless poets. Mine was an immense, formidable brute. He was called by a name which seemed

to me, naturally enough, to sound like Booby, a name which the commander interpreted to be one of the titles of a beautiful woman. But the great, scrawny, bald back

The Camel's Head in Profile.

of his head, and his general rusty toughness and clumsiness, insensibly begat for him in my mind the name of MacWhirter, and by that name he was known so long as I knew him.

10. "The motion of the camel, which is represented as very wearisome, we found to be soothing. The monotonous swing made me intolerably drowsy in the still, warm mornings, and the dragomen tell tales of Howadji who drop asleep as they ride, and who, losing their balance, break arms, legs, and necks, in their fall to the

ground. The tedium of camel-riding is its sluggishness, for although the beasts can trot so that the sultans and the caliphs have dispatched expresses in eight days from Cairo to Damascus, yet the trot of the usual traveling-camel is very hard. The pasha's El Shiraz had a sufficiently pleasant trotting gait; but MacWhirter's exertions in that kind shook my soul within me.

11. "Yet with all this the effect of the motion of the camel, separated from his awkward and ridiculous form and its details, is stately and dignified; so much so, indeed, that the imagination would select him first as the bearer of a dignitary in a pageant. Covered with long, sweeping draperies, which should conceal him entirely, and his rounded hump spread with heavy carpets, he presents a moving throne for a caliph or a sultan in his desert progress of dignity unsurpassed. The rider sits supreme above the animal and over the earth, and the long, languid movement harmonizes with the magnificent monotony of the scene."

12. Bayard Taylor also writes: "I found dromedary-riding not at all difficult. One sits on a very lofty seat, with his feet crossed over the animal's shoulders or resting on his neck. The body is obliged to rock backward and forward on account of the long, swinging gait, and as there is no stay or fulcrum except a blunt pommel, around which the legs are crossed, some little power of equilibrium is necessary. My dromedary was a strong, stately beast of a light cream color, and so even of gait that it would bear the Arab test, that is, one might drink a cup of coffee while going on a full trot without spilling a drop.

13. "I found a great advantage in the use of the Oriental costume. My trousers allowed the legs perfect freedom of motion, and I soon learned so many different

modes of crossing those members that no day was sufficient to exhaust them. The rising and kneeling of the animal is hazardous at first, as his long legs double together like a carpenter's rule, and you are thrown backward and then forward, and then backward again; but the trick is soon learned. The soreness and fatigue of which many travelers complain I never felt, and I attribute much of it to the Frank dress. I rode from eight to ten hours a day, read, and even dreamed in the saddle, and was at night as fresh and unwearied as when I mounted in the morning.

Camels and Arabs.

14. "My caravan was accompanied by four Arabs. They owned the camels, which they urged along with a shrill, barbaric song, the burden of which was, 'O Prophet of God, help the camels and bring them safely to our

journey's end!' They were very susceptible to cold, and a temperature of fifty degrees, which we frequently had in the morning, made them tremble like aspen-leaves, and they were sometimes so benumbed that they could scarcely load the camels. They were proud of their enormous heads of hair, which they wore parted on both temples, the middle portion being drawn into an upright mass six inches in height, while the side divisions hung over the ears in a multitude of little twists.

15. "These love-locks they anointed every morning with suet, and they looked as if they had slept in a hard frost until the heat had melted the fat. I thought to flatter one of them as he performed the operation by exclaiming, 'Beautiful!' but he coolly answered: 'You speak the truth; it is very beautiful.' The Arabs wore long swords carried in a leathern scabbard over the left shoulder, and sometimes favored us with a war-dance, which consisted merely in springing into the air with a brandished sword and turning around once before coming down. They were all very devout, retiring a short distance from the road to say their prayers at the usual hours, and performing the prescribed ablutions with sand instead of water."

CHAPTER XXXVII.

SOME COUSINS OF THE CAMEL.

1. THE llama is an inhabitant of the mountainous regions of Peru and Chili. About the height of a small horse, and possessing some of the characteristics of the sheep, it really belongs, by its structure and use, to the family of the camel. From a remote date it has been to

the Peruvians what the reindeer is to the Lapps or the camel to the merchant of the desert, the one animal of

The Llama of the Andes.

many uses. Besides being a beast of burden, it has furnished the Peruvians with food and clothes.

2. Like the camel, the llama has two toes on each foot; hard caps, or callosities, on its breast; and the peculiar formation of the stomach for storing water. Unlike the camel, its toes are entirely separated, and armed with claws or talons to catch upon smooth surfaces, though on the under side the toes are provided with easy cushions. It is evident that, while the camel is adapted to move on

the sandy plain, the llama is peculiarly suited to rougher and more uneven footing.

3. The llama, and its cousins the alpaca, or paca, and the smaller vicunia, find their most agreeable home on the highly elevated plains or mountain-tables of the Andes. Between eight and twelve thousand feet high is their favorite altitude, and they are apt to suffer or die when compelled to live on lower levels. "The alpaca is a variety of the llama remarkable for the length and fleecy softness of its hair; its head is shorter than that of the llama, and the texture of the fleece is very peculiar, insomuch that for the manufacture of a variety of textile fabrics it has recently become extremely valuable as an article of commerce.

4. "The color of the alpaca is very variable; some individuals are jet-black, others brown, pied, or spotted. The Peruvians do not employ this animal as a beast of burden in their native country, but prize it solely on account of its wool, of which pouches are made. The vicunia, another variety of the same race, is not larger than a sheep; its hair, or rather wool, is extremely soft and so fine as to be employed in the manufacture of the most costly fabrics."

5. An old writer on Peru, in 1544, says: "In places where there is no snow, the natives want water, and to supply this they fill the skins of sheep with water, and make other living sheep carry them; for it must be remarked that these sheep of Peru are large enough to serve as beasts of burden. They can carry about one hundred pounds or more, and the Spaniards used to ride them, and they would go four or five leagues a day. When they are weary they lie down upon the ground, and as there are no means of making them get up, either by beating or assisting them, the load must of necessity be taken off. When

there is a man on one of them, if the beast is tired, and urged to go on, he turns his head around, and discharges his saliva, which has an unpleasant odor, into the rider's face.

6. "These animals are of great use and profit to their masters, for their wool is very good and fine, particularly that of the species called pacas, which have very long fleeces. And the expense of their food is trifling, as a

The Paca.

handful of maize suffices them, and they can go four or five days without water. Their flesh is as good as that of the fat sheep of Castile." These animals were domesticated from a remote antiquity, as is evident from the fact that in the graves of the Incas, the original inhabitants, clothing made from alpaca-wool has been found.

7. Squier, in his descriptive sketches of Peruvian travel, writes: "The merchants of Tacna have built here a rude inclosure for the droves of llamas that come from the interior with products for the coast, and here is also a little cluster of buildings for persons connected with the trade, homely and poor, but a welcome refuge for the tired traveler. As we rode up, a troop of more than a thousand llamas, with proudly-curved necks, erect heads, great, inquiring, timid eyes, and suspicious ears thrust forward to catch the faintest sound of danger, each with its hundred pounds of ore secured in sacks on its back, led, not driven, by quaintly costumed Indians, filed past us into the inclosure of the establishment."

8. "The Spaniards were amazed," says Prescott, "by the number as well as the magnitude of the flocks of llamas which they saw browsing on the stunted herbage that grows in the elevated regions of the Andes. Sometimes they were gathered in inclosures, but more usually were roaming at large under the conduct of their Indian shepherds; and the conquerors now learned, for the first time, that these animals were tended with as much care, and their migrations as nicely regulated, as those of the vast flocks of merinos in their own country.

9. "Of the four varieties of the Peruvian sheep, the llama, the one most familiarly known, is the least valuable on account of its wool. It is chiefly employed as a beast of burden, for which, although it is somewhat larger than any of the other varieties, its diminutive size and strength would seem to disqualify it. It carries a load of little more than a hundred pounds, and can not travel above three or four leagues a day. But all this is compensated by the little care and cost required for its management

and its maintenance. It picks up an easy subsistence from the moss and stunted herbage that grows scantily along the withered sides and steppes of the Cordilleras.

10. "The structure of its stomach enables it to dispense with any supply of water for weeks, nay, months together. Its spongy hoof, armed with a claw or pointed talon to enable it to take secure hold on the ice, never requires to be shod; and the load laid upon its back rests securely in its bed of wool without the aid of girth or saddle. The llamas move in troops of five hundred, or even a thousand, and thus, though each individual carries but little, the aggregate is considerable. The whole caravan travels on at its regular pace, passing the night in the open air, without suffering from the coldest temperature, and marching in perfect order, and in obedience to the voice of the driver."

11. And Hartwick, in "The Tropical World," says: "The llama, and its near relations, the alpaca, the huanacu, and the vicunia, the largest four-footed animals which Peru possessed before the Spaniards introduced the horse or the ox, are all natives of the Puna. Long before the invasion of Pizarro, the llama was used by the Peruvians as a beast of burden, and was not less serviceable to them than the camel to the Arabs of the desert. The wool served for the material of a coarse cloth; the milk and flesh as food; the skin as a warm covering or mantle; and without the assistance of the llama it would have been impossible for the Indians to transport goods or provisions on the high table-lands of the Andes, or for the Incas to have founded and maintained their vast empire.

12. "The llama is also historically remarkable as the only animal domesticated by the aboriginal Americans. The reindeer of the north and the bison of the prairies enjoyed then, as they do now, their savage independence;

the llama alone was obliged to submit to the yoke of man. The Indians often travel with large herds of llamas to the coast to fetch salt. Each day these journeys are very short, for the llamas never feed after sunset, and are thus obliged to graze while journeying, or to rest for several hours. While reposing they utter a peculiar low tone, which at a distance resembles the sound of an Æolian harp.

13. "A loaded herd of llamas traversing the high table-lands affords an interesting spectacle. Slowly and stately they proceed, casting inquisitive glances on every side. On seeing any strange object which excites fears, they immediately scatter in every direction, and their poor drivers have great difficulty to gather the herd. The Indians, who are very fond of these animals, decorate their ears with ribbons, hang little bells about their necks, and always caress them before placing the burden on their back. When one of them drops from fatigue, they kneel at its side and strive to encourage it for further exertion by a profusion of flattering epithets and gentle warnings."

14. The musk-deer, about the size of a half-grown common deer, is remarkable on account of the entire absence of horns, and because, though a ruminant, it has, in the upper jaw of the males, canine teeth. It is a beautiful little creature, inhabiting the mountainous districts of Siberia, China, and Thibet. Its name is derived from the pouch which it carries filled with the perfume of musk.

15. Mr. Wilson says of it: "This persecuted little animal would probably have been left to pass a life of peace and quietness in its native forests, but for the celebrated perfume with which Nature has provided it. Its skin being worthless from its small size, the flesh alone would hold out no inducement to hunt it while larger

game was more easily procurable. An ounce of musk may be considered the average for a full-grown animal.

16. "From the first high ridge above the plains to the limits of the forest on the snowy range, and for perhaps the whole length of the chain of the Himalayas, the musk-deer may be found on every hill of an elevation of above eight thousand feet which is clothed with forest. On the lower ranges it is comparatively a rare animal, being confined to near the summits of the highest hills, as an approach to the colder forests near the snow; but it is nowhere numerous, and its retired and solitary habits make it appear still more rare than it really is."

CHAPTER XXXVIII.

FOOT-HANDED FOXES AND SQUIRRELS.

1. WE are now to make the acquaintance of a singular group of animals. On a hasty glance they would be called four-footed, like many other animals; but they are really foot-handed. Both on their extremities, before and behind, they have fingers and thumbs, which are long, flexible, and prehensile. Their arms, as well as their legs, are long, and this structure adapts them to the climbing of trees, where they are most at home, and where their food is chiefly found. They are awkward walkers on the ground, and with difficulty maintain an upright position on their hind-legs. By their agility and supple limbs they are enabled to imitate many human gestures, and often exhibit caricatures of human beings.

2. The lemur, or fox-headed monkey, is an inhabitant of Madagascar and neighboring islands. In their native

home they live in societies, upon trees, and feed mostly upon fruits. Their head is fox-shaped, their hair is soft

The White-footed Lemur.

and woolly, and they are easily tamed. They are gentle and show affection for those who care for them. "If two lemurs are together in a cage, they sit close, with their tails folded round each other's bodies, so as to form one round ball, from which, when disturbed, two heads make their appearance. They may be kept at liberty in a room, having little of the mischievous disposition of other monkeys. They usually take their food in their hands, but sometimes eat bread without holding it. In drinking, they lap like a dog."

3. The aye-aye, from its appearance, takes a position

midway between the lemur and the squirrel. It is a native of Madagascar, and, when full grown, is about eighteen inches long. The structure of its teeth, made necessary by its habits of life, is quite like that of the squirrel, or rodents. It is strictly nocturnal in its habits, and therefore in its native forest is seldom seen. During the day it sleeps in holes in the ground. Mr. Wallace says: " But its most remarkable character is found in its fore-feet, or hands, the fingers of which are all very long, and armed with sharp, curved claws; but one of them, the second, is wonderfully slender, being not half the thickness of the others. This peculiar structure adapts it to feeding upon small, wood-boring insects.

4. "Its strong feet and sharp claws enable it to cling firmly to the branches of trees, in almost any position; by means of its large, delicate ears, it listens for the sound of the insect gnawing within the branch, and is thus able to fix its exact position; with its powerful, curved, gnawing teeth, it rapidly cuts away the bark and wood, till it exposes the burrow of the insect, most probably the soft larva of some beetle, and then comes into play the extraordinary long, wire-like finger, which enters into the burrow, and, with the sharp, bent claws, brings out the grub.

5. " Here we have a most complex adaptation of different parts and organs, all converging to one special end, that end being the same as is reached by a group of birds, the woodpeckers, in a different way; and it is a most interesting fact that, although woodpeckers abound in all the great continents, they are quite absent from Madagascar. We may, therefore, consider that the aye-aye really occupies the same place in nature, in the forests of this tropical island, as do the woodpeckers in other parts of the world."

6. Professor Owen studied an aye-aye which he held in captivity, and, after feeding it fruits, observed its propensity to gnaw the sides of the cage. He introduced a piece of worm-eaten wood into the cage, and, of the actions of the animal, says: "Presently he came to one of the worm-eaten branches, which he began to examine most attentively, and, bending forward his ears, and applying his nose to the bark, he rapidly tapped the surface with his second finger, as a woodpecker taps a tree, from time to time inserting the end of his finger into the hole. At length he came to a part of the branch which gave out an interesting sound, and began to tear with his strong teeth. He rapidly stripped off the bark, cut into the wood, and exposed the nest of the grub, which he daintily picked out, and conveyed the luscious morsel to his mouth."

The Aye-Aye.

7. The flying-cat, of the East Indian Islands, appears to cousin closely with the bat. There are no thumbs on any of its four limbs, nor are its fingers long, like those of the bat. But its long and slender limbs are connected

by a membrane, widely opened by the limbs, which serves as a parachute, assisting it to spring from tree to tree. It is not able to maintain itself in the air, and hence is not a true flier. Its length is about eighteen inches, and it sleeps during the day, in low hills, which it chooses for its dwelling-place.

The Flying Lemur.

These lemurs feed upon fruits and young leaves, and prey upon plantations of cocoa and palm.

CHAPTER XXXIX.

HOWLERS AND WEEPERS OF AMAZONIAN FORESTS.

1. SOUTH AMERICA may be said to be noted as the home of the monkey tribe. The great forests of the tropical regions are filled with the cries, yells, and roarings, by night and by day, of countless troops of these quadrumana, roaming through the tree-tops. Some of the families are diurnal and some nocturnal, and so the noises never cease. They embrace all sizes, from the big howler down to the tiny marmoset, not larger than a flying-squirrel. They all possess a degree of intelligence and cunning somewhat akin to that of the human species. Nearly all have prehensile tails, which give them the advantage of a

fifth hand in clinging to their frail support, and in swinging from branch to branch.

2. A very striking feature of most South American monkeys is the strong resemblance they bear to the Indians of the forest regions, just as those of Africa are said to resemble the negro, and those of the Indian Archipelago the Malay race. Some of them look so much like Indians that one can not help imagining there exists a near relationship between these tribes of forest-dwellers. Humboldt says of the howler: "The face of this singular monkey is nearly concealed by a sandy, bushy beard, ex-

Ursine Howlers.

tending below and projecting considerably beyond his chin, giving him a very dignified appearance. So striking is their resemblance to the human species that, once having shot one, I almost felt as though I had committed murder. When I raised the poor creature from the ground, upon which he had fallen, his large gray eyes were bathed in tears, and every feature expressed the deepest agony.

3. "Casting upon me a most eloquent look of reproach,

he endeavored to push me aside; but, too much enfeebled by his wound, lay down and calmly resigned himself to the gaze of my English companions, who discussed and disputed about the division of his still panting body—one wanting the skin for a smoking-cap, and the drum of his throat for the bowl of his pipe, while the other would be contented with nothing less than the whole carcass. For my own part, I only desired to get out of sight of the dying creature; and, shouldering my gun, departed in a mood which determined me never again to lift my hand against these innocent wild men of the woods."

4. The largest of the South American monkeys is the ursine howler, named from the loudness of his voice. Wallace gives this description of it: " Often, in the great forests of the Amazon or Orinoco, a tremendous noise is heard in the night or early morning, as if a great assemblage of wild beasts were all roaring and screaming together. The noise may be heard for miles, and it is louder and more piercing than that of any other animals; yet it is all produced by a single male howler, sitting on the branch of some lofty tree. They are able to make this noise by means of an organ possessed by no other animal.

5. " The lower jaw is unusually deep, and this makes room for a hollow, bony vessel, about the size of a large walnut, situated under the root of the tongue, and having an opening into the windpipe, by which the animal can force air into it. This increases the power of its voice, acting something like the hollow case of a violin, and producing those marvelous, rolling sounds, which caused Waterton to declare that they were such as might have had their origin in the infernal regions. The howlers are large and stout-bodied monkeys, with bearded faces, and very strong and powerfully grasping tails. They inhabit the wildest forests. They are very shy, and are seldom

taken captive, though they are less active than many other American monkeys."

The Jaguar among the Howlers.

6. In traveling toward the llanos, south of Caracas, Humboldt came into the neighborhood of these creatures. He says: "The rising of the sun was announced by the distant noise of the howling monkeys. Approaching a group of trees which rise in the midst of the plain, we saw numerous bands of the howlers, moving as if in procession, and very slowly, from one tree to another. A male was followed by a great number of females, several of the latter carrying their young on their shoulders. The howling monkeys live in societies, and everywhere resemble each other, though the species are not always the same. The uniformity with which they perform their movements is extremely striking. Whenever the branches of the trees do not touch each other, the male who leads the party suspends himself by his prehensile tail, and, letting fall the rest of his body, swings himself till, in one of his oscillations, he reaches the neighboring branch. The

whole troop then perform similar movements on the same spot."

7. The spider-monkey consists principally of limbs

Spider-Monkeys.

and tail, the body being comparatively small. It is the most active of all the monkey tribes, and with its long arms and clinging tail it can carry its light body through the tree-tops with surprising rapidity. They are gentle and timid, and, when not frightened, they are slow and deliberate in their movements. They sometimes are made household pets in their native regions, but, for two reasons, they never can be tolerated like the cat and dog; and these are, their propensity for destructive mischief and their unpleasant and unseemly habits.

8. Paez gives this description of them : "These monkeys are very destructive of cocoa-plantations and corn-fields. When about to commence their depredations, they usually assemble in great numbers and exercise many precautions. The first step is to station several of their number as sentinels upon the highest trees overlooking the avenues leading to the plantation, to give warning of approaching danger. The next proceeding is that of placing the females and young, who can not take part in the foray, in some safe retreat. They then invest the corn-field in earnest, pulling down the stalks and tearing off the ears of corn with astonishing rapidity, chattering, laughing, and yelling all the while, like a set of mischievous schoolboys in the absence of the master.

9. "When they have obtained a sufficient number of ears, they split the husks, and tie them in pairs by means of a peculiar knot which in consequence is called a 'monkey-tie.' They then throw the ears across their backs, and hasten to hide their booty in some safe place in the depths of the forest. It often happens that they are surprised by the owner of the corn-field, who suddenly appears and pours a shower of shot into their midst. Then, with shrill cries of alarm, the whole troop scamper off helter-skelter, tumbling, pitching, or hobbling on all-fours, but never dropping a particle of their plunder. It is generally believed in the llanos that, after such a surprise,

the careless sentinels are tried by a council of elders, and, if found guilty, they are tied to a tree and soundly whipped.

10. "No less remarkable is their method of crossing streams which they encounter in the forest. The strongest of the party climbs to the spreading branches of some tree projecting over the stream. He then twists his tail firmly around a branch, and, letting his body hang below, seizes upon the tail of the next, and so on until a long chain is formed. By pushing, as in a swing, the living pendulum sweeps across the stream, the last monkey seizing a branch on the other side. On this bridge the whole troop passes, and the members which formed the bridge are helped over or pulled through by their companions. Sometimes one or more lose their lives, which has given rise to a proverb, 'It is the last monkey that is drowned.'

11. "Sagacious as these animals are, it is easy to entrap them. One of the simplest ways is to cut a number of holes in a gourd, barely large enough to admit the monkey's hand. The gourd is then filled with corn and fastened to the trunk of a tree. Shaking the gourd is a dinner-bell for the monkeys, who no sooner hear the sound than they descend in great numbers to secure the prize. Each in turn thrusts his hand into the gourd and grasps a handful of corn. But in vain do they struggle to withdraw their hands without giving up the prize; and at this moment the trapper makes his appearance, and, tying their hands, carries them off to his cottage in the woods."

12. Another naturalist gives this account of a pet spider-monkey which accompanied him on his journey: "Jerry was a favorite with all, and in all respects fared like ourselves. Its favorite food was farina, boiled rice, and bananas. A raw egg was a choice morsel, and, on being given to it, it broke one end by gently knocking it

on the floor, and completed the hole by picking off the broken bits of shell. It then threw back its head, raised the egg by its two hands, and sucked out its contents. On our journey, Jerry always rode on the back of a large mastiff dog, and in this manner traveled several thousand miles. The two animals were much attached to each other, and it was an amusing sight to see them gamboling together. Before starting, the dog would go every morning to where the monkey was tied, and wait till it was put upon his back, and its cord made fast to his collar. In traveling, it was not particular as to whether its face was toward the head or tail of its charger, except in going down-hill, when its face was turned forward, and, to prevent itself from slipping over the dog's head, it made use of his prehensile tail, curling it around the dog's tail like a crupper."

13. The weepers are smaller and more hairy than the monkeys already described. They have long tails, prehensile only at the extremity, so that they use this limb more as a staff than as a hand. They are named from a plaintive cry which resembles the weeping voice of children. They are timid, living on the tree-tops of retired forests. Their food is seeds, grain, insects, and the eggs of birds. They are

The Marmoset.

gentle and easily tamed. There are at least fourteen distinct species belonging to this family.

14. The marmoset is but little larger than a squirrel, and has a head very much like a fox. It is covered with long, silken hair, and has a bushy tail of moderate length. This tail is not prehensile. Its food is insects and fruits. Humboldt's tame marmoset used to sit by him and inspect his drawings. Pictures of spiders and flies he tried to catch in his paws, but he turned from the picture of a wasp in great terror.

CHAPTER XL.

LONG-TAILED DWELLERS OF THE TREE-TOPS.

1. AMONG the monkeys of the Old World there are some that have long tails and melancholy, solemn-looking countenances. Their tails are of no special use to them in holding or catching the branches of trees. When young they are easily tamed; but after they have grown old they are cross and often vicious. A curious species is the proboscis-monkey, remarkable on account of its long nose, which in the male turns down and in the female turns up. This nose gives them a ludicrous expression. They are found in great numbers in the forests of Borneo, and the natives believe them to be men who have run to the woods to avoid paying tribute.

2. The bonnet-monkey is frequently brought to Europe for exhibition. It is about the size of a large cat, of greenish color, with a long tail. In Bengal it does great injury to fields and gardens. The natives forbid any one to kill it. When young the bonnet-monkey is amusing in confinement, performing all sorts of antics with a look of

solemn gravity. When two or three are kept together, they are constantly hugging and fondling each other.; and,

Proboscis-Monkeys.

when a monkey of this kind has no companion of its own species, it will pet a kitten and almost choke it with its fond attention.

3. The common baboon is an inhabitant of the hottest part of Africa, and grows to three and even four feet high. He is more ferocious than others of the monkey tribe, and is not so often tamed. His general color is

grayish-brown. The face is of a tawny flesh-color, with a tuft of hair on each side and surmounted by a large bunch, giving the animal a ludicrous appearance. Baboons abound in Siam, where they frequently sally forth in multitudes to attack the villages when the peasants are busy in the rice-harvest, and plunder their habitations of whatever provisions they can lay their paws on. Fruit, corn, and roots are their usual food, though they will also eat flesh.

4. "The army of Alexander the Great marched in complete battle array into a country inhabited by great numbers of baboons and encamped there for the night. The next morning, when the army was about to proceed on its march, the soldiers saw at some distance an enormous number of baboons drawn up in rank and file like a small army with such regularity, that the Macedonians, who could have no idea of such a manœuvre, imagined at first that it was the enemy drawn up to receive them."

The Baboon.

5. The hoonuman, or entellus monkey, is venerated by the Hindoos, who believe that if any person kills one he will die within a year. This monkey is about three feet high, has a yellowish body, and black face and hands. The hair above the eyebrows forms an odd projection,

and there is a tuft of beard on the chin. "These monkeys, being protected from injury by the superstition of the Hindoos, become a perfect nuisance to those who

The Entellus.

have no veneration for them. They take their abode in groves or trees which are planted about villages, and sometimes are so numerous as to outnumber the human inhabitants of the place.

6. "Sir J. Forbes says that at Dhuboy the roofs of the houses seemed entirely appropriated to the monkeys, and gives a humorous account of having been obliged to take shelter in a veranda because these animals pelted him with tiles and mortar from an opposite house. They are mischievous and destructive, and will strip a corn-field of moderate size in a few hours. They frequently, however, destroy poisonous snakes. They seize them by the neck when asleep, and, running to the nearest stone, grind the head by a strong friction on the surface, frequently

looking at it and grinning. When convinced that the venomous fangs are destroyed, they toss the reptile to their young ones to play with, and seem to rejoice in the destruction of their common enemy."

7. The gibbons, or long-armed apes, are natives of Southern Asia and the adjacent islands. Mr. Wallace says: "They are generally of small size and of a gentle disposition, but possessing the most wonderful agility. In these creatures the arms are as long as the body and legs together, and are so powerful that a gibbon will hang for hours suspended from a branch, or will swing to-and-fro, and then throw itself a great distance through the air. The arms, in fact, completely take the place of legs in traveling.

8. "Instead of jumping from bough to bough, and running on the branches, like other apes and monkeys, the gibbons move along while suspended in the air, stretching their arms from bough to bough, and thus going hand over hand, as a very active sailor will climb along a rope. The strength of the arms is, however, so prodigious, and their hold so sure, that they often loose one hand before they have caught a bough with the other, thus seeming almost to fly through the air by a series of swinging leaps; and they travel among the net-work of interlacing boughs, a hundred feet above the earth, with as much ease and certainty as we walk or run upon level ground, and with even greater speed.

9. "These little animals scarcely ever come down to the ground of their own accord; but, when obliged to do so, they run along almost erect, with their long arms swinging round and round, as if trying to find some tree or other object to climb upon. They are the only apes who naturally walk without using their hands as well as their feet; but this does not make them move like men,

for it is evident that the attitude is not an easy one, and it is only adopted because the arms are habitually used to swing by, and are, therefore, naturally held upward instead of downward, as they must be when walking on them."

CHAPTER XLI.

TAILLESS TREE-CLIMBERS OF THE WILDS.

1. Of the gorilla, Du Chaillu says: "My long residence in Africa gave me superior facilities for intercourse with the natives, and, as my curiosity was greatly excited

The Gorilla at Home.

by the reports of this unknown monster, I was determined to penetrate to its haunts and see with my own eyes. It has been my fortune to be the first white man who can speak of the gorilla from personal knowledge; and while my experience and observation prove that many of the actions reported of it are false, I can also vouch that no description can exceed the horror of its appearance, the ferocity of its attack, or the impish malignity of its nature. It lives in the loneliest and darkest portions of the dense African jungle, preferring deep-wooded valleys and also rugged heights.

2. "It is a restless and nomadic beast, wandering from place to place, and scarce ever found for two days together in the same neighborhood. In part this restlessness is caused by the struggle it has to find its favorite food, which consists of berries, pineapples, and other vegetable matter. The gorilla, though it has immense canine teeth and though its vast strength fits it to capture and kill almost every animal which frequents the forest, is a strict vegetarian. The common walk of this animal is not on its hind-legs, but on all-fours. In this posture the arms are so long that the head and breast are raised considerably, and as it runs the hind-legs are brought far beneath the body. The leg and arm on the same side move together, which gives the beast a curious waddle. It can run at great speed. It is a pretty sight to see a mother with the baby gorilla sporting with it. I have watched them in the wood till I had not the heart to shoot. When the mother runs away from the hunter, the young one grasps her about the neck and hangs beneath her breasts with its legs about her body.

3. "In all my hunts and encounters with this animal I never knew a grown male to run off. Sitting for a moment with a savage frown on his face, he slowly rises to his

feet, and, looking with glowing and malign eyes at the intruder, begins to beat his breast, and lifting up his round head utters his frightful roar. I have reason to believe that I have heard this roar at a distance of three miles. In shooting the hippopotamus at night, the negro always scampers off as soon as he has fired his gun. When he has fired at the gorilla, he stands still. I asked why they did not run in this case too, and was answered that it would be of no use. To run was fatal. One blow of that huge paw with its bony claws, and the hunter is finished."

4. The orang-outang is a native of Sumatra and Borneo. The adult measures about six and a half feet in height. His head is covered with a coat of thick, coarse, blackish hair. He has a naked face, a tufted mustache on the upper lip, and a long, reddish beard. The orangs have little fear of man, but, if pursued, will climb the highest trees and throw down upon their pursuers a shower of sticks.

Young Orang-Outang.

5. The orang inhabits the wild forests of uncultivated districts, where he is known to the natives by the name of *mias*. Mr. Wallace says: "It is a singular and most interesting sight to watch a mias making his way

leisurely through the forest. He walks deliberately along the branches, in the semi-erect attitude which the great length of his arms and the shortness of his legs give him. Choosing a place where the boughs of an adjacent tree intermingle, he seizes the smaller twigs, pulls them toward him, grasps them, together with those of the tree he is on, and thus forming a kind of bridge swings himself onward, and, seizing hold of a thick branch with his long arms, is in an instant walking along the opposite side of the tree. He never jumps or springs, or even appears to hurry himself, and yet moves as quickly as a man can run along the ground beneath.

Bornean Orang.

6. "The enemies of the orang are few in number. The Dyaks are unanimous in their statements that the mias never either attacks or is attacked by any animal, with one exception, which is highly curious, and would be hardly credible were it not confirmed by the testimony of several independent parties who have been eye-witnesses of the circumstance. The only animal the mias measures his strength with is the crocodile. The account of the natives is as follows: 'When there is little fruit in the jungle, the mias goes to the river-side to eat the fruits that grow there, and also the young shoots of some palm-trees which are found on the water's edge. The crocodile

then sometimes tries to seize him; but he gets on to the reptile's back, beats it with his hands and feet on the head and neck, and pulls open its jaws till he rips up the throat. The mias always kills the crocodile, for he is very strong; there is no animal in the jungle so strong as he.'"

7. The chimpanzee has been regarded as nearest like man of any of the foot-handed animals; but between the two there are some points of remarkable difference in structure. The length of the arms in the chimpanzee is such that, with his legs slightly bent, his fingers touch the ground. The hands are awkward as hands, and the feet are not adapted for easy standing or walking. This animal is at home on the western coasts of Africa. It is readily tamed, and has attracted attention by its simple and refined manners.

Hand of Chimpanzee.

Foot of Chimpanzee.

8. The chimpanzee, in intelligence and kindliness of disposition, ranks higher than any other of the foot-handed tenants of the trees. In its native wilds it builds a kind of leafy nest among the boughs of the loftiest trees. This nest is made up of small

interlaced branches, well thatched with leaves, and impenetrable to water; fixed by firmly-tied bands, it is generally from six to eight feet in diameter, and presents the form of a dome, an arrangement which readily throws off the rain. The male and the female share in the building of the hut; but the female and her young alone occupy it, the male remaining outside. The nests, in shape and manner of structure, are very much like those of the savages who inhabit the same region.

9. Dr. Brehm, the German naturalist, says: "It is really impossible to treat the chimpanzee like an animal; his character and general behavior show so much of humanity that men are induced to commune with him in the same way as with their equals. In captivity he is perfectly conscious of his position, and subordinates himself willingly to the superior mental gifts and capacities of mankind, but holds himself better and higher than other animals, especially than other monkeys. Paying, in every instance, high regard to men, he likes children if they do not tease and molest him. Sportive and humorous, he indulges in joking with men and animals.

10. "He is not only inquisitive, but eager to acquire knowledge, examines carefully things strange to him, and falls into ecstasy when he has found out their purpose and learned to use them in the right way. While able to understand men and things, he is nevertheless modest and kindly, seldom willful, and never stubborn, although he claims what is in right due to him. Of variable temper, he is now good-humored and jolly, now sad and morose, and gives vent to his feelings as men do, but sometimes in a more passionate way.

11. "I was once the owner of a highly-educated chimpanzee. He knew all the friends of the house, all our acquaintances, and distinguished them readily from stran-

gers. Every one treating him kindly he looked upon as a personal friend. He never felt more comfortable than when he was admitted to the family circle, and allowed to move freely around, and open and shut doors, while his joy was boundless when he was assigned a place at the common table, and the guests admired his natural wit and practical jokes. He expressed his satisfaction and thanks to them by drumming furiously on the table.

12. "In his numerous moments of leisure his favorite occupation consisted in investigating carefully every object in his reach; he lowered the door of the stove for the purpose of watching the fire, opened drawers, rummaged boxes and trunks, and played with their contents, provided the latter did not look suspicious to him. How easily suspicion was aroused in him might be illustrated by the fact that, as long as he lived, he shrank with terror from every rubber ball. Obedience to my orders, and attachment to my person, and to everybody caring for him, were among his cardinal virtues, and he bored me with his persistent wishes to accompany me.

13. "He knew perfectly his time for retiring, and was happy when some one of us carried him to the bedroom like a baby. As soon as the light was put out, he would jump into the bed and cover himself, because he was afraid of the darkness. His favorite meal was supper, with tea, which he was very fond of, provided it was largely sweetened and mixed with rum. He sipped it from the cup, and ate the dipped bread-slices with a spoon, having been taught not to use his fingers in eating; he poured his wine from the bottle, and drank it from the glass. A man could hardly behave better at table than did that monkey.

14. "He was especially engaging in his association with my children, always gentle, obliging, and tender, and

they liked him as a good fellow and pretty playmate. When he was first introduced to my little girl, who was then six months old, he seemed perplexed, and observed her with astonishment, as if speculating whether that little bit of a creature was really a human being. At last his mind was made up; he touched her cheek with one finger, and then offered her his hand in friendship. My chimpanzee conversed very little with other animals; like the apes in general, he was afraid of the big ones, and despised the smaller ones. He was always around us, and we, on our side, did not make any difference between him and a man.

15. "The animal fell ill of the mumps, followed by pneumonia. I had seen many sick chimpanzees, but never one of them behaved as he did. I engaged two competent physicians to take charge of him. He knew them from the first day, allowed them to feel his pulse, showed his tongue, and directed the hand of the attendant doctor to the painful swelling, which had to be cut open afterward, there being danger of suffocation.

16. "The doctors would not use chloroform, out of regard to the affection of the lungs; but, fearing the chimpanzee would not keep quiet during the operation, engaged four strong men to hold him. The sick animal did not submit to that rough treatment, but excitedly pushed the men aside, and then, without any compulsion whatever, but in compliance with the fondling words of his nurse, in whose lap he was sitting, offered his throat. The operation was performed, the ape never flinching or complaining. He felt afterward much relieved, and expressed his gratitude by pressing fervently the hands of the physicians and kissing his nurse."

REMUS CROWLEY AND HIS HABITS.

1. During the winter most of the animals of the Central Park menagerie are carefully housed; only a few which are accustomed to cold winters remain where they are seen in the summer. The chimpanzee, Remus Crowley, Esq., occupies a cage in the office of Superintendent Conklin. A temperature between sixty and seventy degrees is maintained at all times, and the animal is as carefully protected from all draughts as an invalid person. In his native climate of Liberia cold draughts are unknown, and when exposed to them Mr. Crowley pays the penalty with a sore throat or a cold in the head. At night a heavy blanket is placed in his cage, and when the weather is extremely cold he wraps himself up in it, but at other times uses it as a mattress. "Jake," a robust park official, attends to him regularly, and the strongest attachment exists between them.

The Chimpanzee.

2. In personal appearance, Mr. Crowley has nothing delicate about him. He came to the Central Park last June, and has now entered on his third year, growing rapidly and gaining over a pound a month; if he lives several years longer, he will probably attain a height of five feet. At present he is a trifle over two feet high, and weighs twenty-six pounds. His hair is parted in the middle, and banged on his forehead; his body is covered heavily with hair and has no tail. When he stands upright, Mr. Crowley presents fully as civilized an appearance as the man in a heavy fur coat who crowds himself in a narrow

place in the street-car. His hands are shriveled and brown, but his nails are delicately tinted and well-shaped, though evidently not looked after by a manicure, and his feet have characteristics resembling those in human feet, except that they are more flexible, and he uses them as readily as he does his hands.

3. "Jake," said Mr. Conklin, "we will have lunch if it is Mr. Crowley's time." "Jake" placed some bananas on a low table, and then a plate, cup and saucer, and knife and fork. After setting out an infant's chair with a cushion in it, he led by the hand the chimpanzee, who had been watching him with apparent satisfaction. Mr. Crowley sprang quickly into the chair and waited patiently while "Jake" pushed him up to the table and placed a pink shawl on his shoulders. "Will you have a banana, old boy?" asked "Jake." Mr. Crowley passed over his plate and received one that had been peeled for him. He picked up his knife and fork carefully and cut a large piece from the fruit and transferred it on the fork to his mouth. "Too much," said "Jake," disapprovingly; "don't be greedy, Crowley."

4. Mr. Crowley cut the slices of the fruit into smaller pieces and ate them deliberately. When "Jake" proposed a glass of milk, he nodded his head with a pleased grin, sipped the milk with a tea-spoon, and then, lifting the cup to his mouth, drank a portion of it. His napkin is embroidered with the name "Remus Crowley," and, after drinking, the chimpanzee wiped his broad mouth and chin with it fastidiously. But having finished his meal, he held out his plate for more, and, when refused, protruded his lower lip and cried disconsolately. Then he shook hands with the visitors, examined their finger-rings and pockets curiously, and, when returned to his cage with reluctance, made faces at all present, and occa-

sionally threw a handful of sawdust at them and danced boisterously.

5. "He is good-natured and as playful as a child," said Mr. Conklin, "not malicious, but full of mischief, and understands everything that goes on around him. In fact, he often reminds me of a deaf and dumb child or an idiot." "Does he make any sound indicating speech?" "No; he utters peculiar cries and moves his lips at times as a person would in talking. He shows clearly the different emotions of anger, pain, and grief, sulks when offended and laughs when pleased. My belief in evolution has increased since I have had him under my care. I have seen many human beings less intelligent, and I believe that with careful selection for breeding there is strong possibility that the race might be developed and taught to speak. It certainly would be an interesting experiment, and would probably require several generations."

New York Tribune, 1884.

THE END.

www.ingramcontent.com/pod-product-compliance
Lightning Source LLC
Chambersburg PA
CBHW021408230426
43666CB00006B/672